marina city

Bristol Public Library

marina city
bertrand goldberg's
urban vision

igor marjanović and katerina rüedi ray

Princeton Architectural Press · New York

← *previous*

View from across the Chicago River, Marina City (1959–1967), Bertrand Goldberg Associates Chicago, IL, ca. 1965. Hedrich-Blessing [photographer], HB-23215-D5, Chicago History Museum.

Published by
Princeton Architectural Press
37 East 7th Street
New York, NY 10003

For a free catalog of books call
1-800-722-6657
Visit our website at www.papress.com

This publication was supported by a grant from
the Graham Foundation for Advanced Studies in
the Fine Arts.

Editor: Wendy Fuller
Designer: Paul Wagner

Special thanks to: Nettie Aljian, Bree Anne Apperley,
Sara Bader, Nicola Bednarek, Janet Behning,
Becca Casbon, Carina Cha, Tom Cho, Penny (Yuen Pik) Chu,
Carolyn Deuschle, Russell Fernandez, Pete Fitzpatrick,
Jan Haux, Linda Lee, Laurie Manfra, John Myers,
Katharine Myers, Dan Simon, Andrew Stepanian,
Jennifer Thompson, Joseph Weston, and Deb Wood of
Princeton Architectural Press —Kevin C. Lippert, publisher

Library of Congress Cataloging-in-Publication Data
Marjanovic, Igor.
Marina City : Bertrand Goldberg's urban vision /
Igor Marjanović and Katerina Rüedi Ray. — 1st ed.
    p.   cm.
Includes index.
ISBN 978-1-56898-863-4 (alk. paper)
1. Marina City (Chicago, Ill.) 2. Goldberg, Bertrand,
1913–1997–Criticism and interpretation. 3. Skyscrapers–
Illinois–Chicago. 4. Architecture–Illinois–Chicago–History–
20th century.
5. Chicago (Ill.)–Buildings, structures, etc. I. Rüedi, Katerina.
II. Title. III. Title: Bertrand Goldberg's urban vision.
NA6233.C4M376 2010
720'.483092–dc22
                                           2009034120

contents

acknowledgments

Many people supported our work on this book.

We are grateful to Washington University in St. Louis and Bowling Green State University who generously supported this project and provided an intellectually stimulating environment in which our work was encouraged and appreciated.

The production of this book was generously supported by the Graham Foundation for Advanced Studies in the Fine Arts. We are grateful to the foundation for placing their trust in us and for helping us in this important undertaking.

The publication of this book would not have been possible without the dedication and support of staff members at various archives around the world. We are indebted to Mary Woolever, Nathaniel Parks, and Danielle Kramer of the Art Institute of Chicago Ryerson and Burnham Libraries and Lori Boyer of the Art Institute of Chicago Department of Architecture. Their knowledge of the Bertrand Goldberg Collection, and their kindness and efficiency, helped us during our frequent visits to the Art Institute of Chicago. We are also grateful to Rob Medina of the Chicago History Museum for his generosity and help with the Hedrich-Blessing Archives. Louis Jones of the Walter P. Reuther Library of Labor and Urban Affairs at Wayne State University provided invaluable help and support in navigating the archives of the Service Employees International Union. Laura Muir and Christopher Linnane of the Busch-Reisinger Museum Archive at Harvard University and Sabine Hartmann of the Bauhaus-Archiv Berlin assisted us with images of Bertrand Goldberg's Bauhaus work.

We are also indebted to many companies and individuals who generously granted and assisted with image permission rights for this book: Gustavo Amaris of Severud Associates, Joseph Rosa of the Art Institute of Chicago,

Ward Miller of the Richard Nickel Committee, Kiyonori Kikutake, Charles Kirman, Elizabeth Bacom, Diane Korling, Steven Kalette, Sara Beck, Kaori Omura, Laura Negri, Lisa Lanspery, Peter Pedraza, Nicholas Boyarsky, Sharon Dennis, Walter Wojtowicz, and Wilco's manager Tony Margherita and his public relations representative Deb Bernardini, all of whom provided important images for this book. Finally, we are also grateful to Gina Grafos of Washington University in St. Louis who helped us with image files and their preparation for printing.

We benefited enormously from Bertrand Goldberg's son Geoffrey Goldberg's breadth and depth of knowledge of the project materials, as well as his recollections of working with his father. Bertold Weinberg's impressive memory of Marina City's design and construction from 1958 to 1963 was of incomparable help. Louis Rocah from the University of Illinois at Chicago shared his experiences as a Goldberg employee in the office and on the Marina City building site. David Dunster from the University of Liverpool, who worked for Bertrand Goldberg Associates as an intern, also provided important information. We are truly grateful for their insights.

We also wish to thank David Van Zanten of Northwestern University and Roberta Feldman of the University of Illinois at Chicago for their support.

Students at the Sam Fox School of Design and Visual Arts at Washington University in St. Louis who participated in the Marina City seminar made important contributions to this book and their insightful feedback provided additional encouragement for our work. At Bowling Green State University Candace Ducat was essential to the completion of this book.

We offer our sincere thanks to Princeton Architectural Press and their dedicated staff. Jennifer Thompson's enthusiasm for this project and her perceptive criticism helped shape this book. Our editor Wendy Fuller has been a wonderfully thorough, insightful, and supportive partner in this project.

We are grateful to our families and friends who aided our work tirelessly. Petar Tomičić, Leah Ray, Kevin Grzyb, and Michelle Storrs Booz provided regular and much needed support during our frequent visits to Chicago.

Finally, we would like to thank Jasna Marjanović and Roger Ray. This book was their project too; it would have been impossible without their love and support.

introduction

BUT MOST VISITORS WILL PREFER TO MAKE FOR THE SYMBOL OF THE CHICAGO THAT IS AND WILL BE: THE TWIN TOWERS OF BERTRAND GOLDBERG'S MARINA CITY, FAR FROM PERFECTED IN DETAIL BUT SO HEROIC IN CONCEPTION, SO RIGHT FOR THEIR SITE WHERE DEARBORN CROSSES THE RIVER, THAT THEY HAVE THE AUTHORITY OF A SKETCH FOR A POSSIBLE THIRD PHASE IN THE HISTORY OF THE CHICAGO SCHOOL.

—REYNER BANHAM, "A WALK IN THE LOOP"

With these words regarding Marina City—a pioneering mixed-use complex on the north bank of the Chicago River—the influential British architecture critic Reyner Banham envisioned a new heroic period of Chicago's architecture. This book examines Marina City, probing its origins, production, and afterlife, and reevaluates its position as an iconic project of twentieth-century architecture. Through the combined efforts of its architect Bertrand Goldberg, client and union leader William McFetridge, and realtor and later Chicago Housing Authority chairman Charles Swibel, Marina City introduced new ideas about form, structure, living, and working, relying on innovative urban, political, financial, construction, and marketing strategies to do so. Commissioned by the Building Service Employees International Union, colloquially known as the Janitor's Union, Marina City was a "house that janitors built"—a true merger of formal and social ideals associated with what is often loosely called midcentury modernism.[1] Commissioned in 1959, the complex broke ground in November 1960. Its most recognizable features, the twin residential towers, were finished in 1963 and 1964; the office building and the theater building were completed in late 1964 and 1967 respectively. The book will examine this period of Marina City's design, construction, and early reception.[2]

While this volume focuses on a single building complex, it includes a broader discussion of the cultural and socioeconomic contexts of architectural production—in line with Goldberg's own passion for historical, economic, social, and cultural knowledge. Goldberg wrote about cities as cultural artifacts, blending a modernist sensibility for social action with traditional ideas of urbanism, humanism, and public space. His ability to think across space and time was

←
1. Bertrand Goldberg, portrait, Chicago office, 1952. Torkel Korling [photographer]. By permission of Diane Korling. Bertrand Goldberg Archive, Ryerson and Burnham Archives, The Art Institute of Chicago. Digital File #200203.081229-652 © The Art Institute of Chicago.

particularly evident in his integration of ideas from the European avant-garde and the U.S. market-driven building economy—a tempering of idealism with realism that led to the urban vision of Marina City.

In addressing these broader themes, this book documents not only the architecture of Marina City but also the complexity of architectural skills and partnerships needed for its realization. It includes previously unpublished drawings, photographs, and documents from the Art Institute of Chicago's Bertrand Goldberg Collection and the Walter P. Reuther Library of Labor and Urban Affairs at Wayne State University, only recently available for public study. These sources help position Marina City not only within architectural, political, and socioeconomic contexts of its time but also in relation to its historical reception within architectural and popular culture.

Marina City entered architectural discourse swiftly; even before it was completed in 1967 many architects, historians, and construction industry professionals around the world saw it as an important building. Carl Condit, Chicago's noted architectural historian, wrote in 1964 about Marina City in *The Chicago School of Architecture* and later in *Chicago, 1930–70: Building, Planning, and Urban Technology*, identifying its importance in Chicago's architectural and civic culture. Yet many other writings focused mainly on its technological history, structural systems, and architectural form. Without enough attention to the genesis, finance, program, development, and reception of buildings, this approach remained formalist, canonizing the so-called Chicago School of architecture through often-superficial analyses, such as corner shots of buildings.[3]

Despite Marina City's initial visibility in the professional and popular press—an important phenomenon—it received relatively little long-term attention in mainstream architectural criticism. It reemerged briefly with the publication of a bilingual exhibition catalog titled *Goldberg: Dans la Ville / On the City* accompanying a major retrospective of Goldberg's work at the Paris Art Center in 1985. Edited by Michel Ragon, the monograph represents the most comprehensive overview of Goldberg's work to date. With a preface by curator Ante Glibota, essays by Ragon and Goldberg, and many iconic photographs of Goldberg's buildings by Hedrich-Blessing, Orlando Cabanban, and other photographers, this image-heavy book provided an important overview of the architect's lifework. Goldberg's essays—"Rich is Right" and "The Critical Mass of Urbanism"—are important accounts of his interest in the city, community, and social space embodied in the Marina City complex.[4] Goldberg's emphasis on urban culture is one of the reasons that we named this book *Marina City: Bertrand Goldberg's Urban Vision*. This title, however, speaks to another important aspect of Marina City—its high visibility and optical sophistication. Its round balconies and roof decks were cameralike devices for viewing the city, yet they were also an object of urban gaze and quickly became symbols of Chicago itself. Thus, the word *vision* in the title refers both to Marina City's optical qualities and to its urban idealism.

Our approach to Marina City builds upon the work of Condit and Ragon but also charts a new path in its critical reception. Unlike Condit or Ragon we had the benefit of greater historical distance, allowing us to examine Marina City more closely within the context of twentieth-century U.S. history, including its relationship to the Great Depression, World War II, and the Cold War. We argue that Marina City, though a uniquely Chicago building, was a product of these larger contexts. Historical distance has also allowed us to address the reception of Marina City, including some of the criticisms that it received.

We also had the benefit of newly available archives that allowed us to examine these issues with greater specificity.

The result of our research is a combination of monograph, historical documentary, and critical overview. This book is structured in six chapters and an epilogue documenting Marina City's origin, construction, reception, and afterlife. It begins with a prologue, a fictional first encounter with Marina City in the 1960s by an imagined typical resident. The chapters "Before Marina City" and "Unpacking Marina City," together with the chapter "Rewrapping Marina City" and the epilogue, frame the book's three central essays on its architecture, finance, and marketing.

"Before Marina City" presents Bertrand Goldberg's personal and professional history up to Marina City, including the role of his teachers and mentors at the Bauhaus and in Chicago. "Unpacking Marina City" introduces the project's key figures—the architect, client, and developer—describing the spaces and programs of the complex and the process of its creation. "The Structure" focuses on the design, engineering, and construction of the complex, including its innovative structural and environmental systems and ambitious construction management. "The Deal" documents Marina City as a political and real estate investment by a labor union, probing the innovative financing that made it possible. "The Image" examines the project's printed materials, showrooms, and extensive media coverage as marketing strategies for and responses to multiple audiences, from political and financial decision-makers to architects, residents, and the general public. "Rewrapping Marina City" turns to the architectural and popular reception of the complex, exploring its legacy in the history of modernist architecture. The epilogue revisits some of the book's main themes and discusses them within the historical, economic, social, and cultural frameworks of the second half of the twentieth century.

Throughout our study, even as we contextualize Marina City, we regularly return our focus to the role of the architect and his relationship to the project partners and their priorities. As images and documents in this volume will attest, Goldberg's architectural, financial, and promotional strategies for Marina City, if sometimes uneven, were highly effective. They raise important questions about the role of design in everyday life as well as the role of the architect in the production of buildings. Yet we were also well aware of the problematic tendency of modernist architectural history to elevate the architect as a hero transforming the built environment; we therefore emphasize Goldberg as part of a complex team of professional and political actors. Nevertheless, we were repeatedly reminded by primary sources that in the midcentury United States his professional standing often gave him a leadership role in such teams.

This book is a record of voices, as they emerged through archival materials, official and unofficial records, and interviews. Yet, many voices involved in the making of architectural modernism were unheard and unrecorded. Like other projects of its magnitude, Marina City had a relatively clear architectural and socioeconomic agenda, yet on issues relating to identity politics—including race, gender, and globalization—its documents remain relatively silent. We hope that subsequent scholars will probe these silences with the great care that they deserve.

Our book instead dissects Marina City as a confluence of design and social action. By examining the complex in this light we hope to illuminate broader architectural themes that speak to architecture's potential as an agent of urban and social change.

prologue

Below is a fictional account of a first encounter with Marina City in the 1960s—prior to later alterations—experienced by an imagined typical resident, based on archival research and one author's life in the complex. Its photographs span five decades, showing key spaces through which Marina City revealed itself to the city and future tenants.

I turn onto Wacker Drive along the calm river speckled with ice. Across the river I glimpse Marina City for the first time. The towers rise above the city sky-line, the winter sky casting deep shadows on the towers' ramps and balconies. [Fig. 2] *The Marina City complex rises from the horizontal plane of the river in sheer—if still restrained—exuberance. I walk to it, and the towers now loom above me as I crane my neck upward, paying respect.* [Fig. 3]

Looking down again, I see the river reflected in the sheerness of a glass plane stretching one floor above the water, from one edge of the site to the other. A momentary gust of wind creates a myriad of flickerings of reflected sunlight—dissolving solidity. For a split second the towers float on a sea of quicksilver.

Before my business, I explore. I rush up the ramp to the plaza level. On my left and right I see rings of trapezoidal columns. Cars arrive, stop, others are already there, waiting; valets arrive jangling keys, get in, and as I watch—riveted—an astonishingly fast drive up the parking ramps takes place, even as other cars drive down at more deliberate speed. Other valets step onto a moving vertical conveyor belt rising upward to waiting cars. I walk to the edge of the plaza—the solid concrete at the river's edge steadies me as I look into the calm, deep-green Chicago River. With cars moving behind me for a moment I nevertheless feel as if I am on a ship, the water moving under me, and I across it.

←

3. View of balconies, Marina City
(1959–1967), Bertrand Goldberg
Associates, Chicago, IL, 2008.

4. Office building, Marina City (1959–
1967), Bertrand Goldberg Associates,
Chicago, IL, 1964. Orlando Cabanban
[photographer]. Bertrand Goldberg Archive, Ryerson
and Burnham Archives, The Art Institute of Chicago.
Digital File #200203.081229-328 © The Art Institute
of Chicago.

I raise my eyes and before me, displayed like an endlessly tall and broad cinema screen, is the architectural panorama of the north edge of the Loop. Chicago.

I walk back toward the center of the plaza. In front of and above me a broad facade appears eerily abstract, almost unreal. [Fig. 4] Its regular rhythm is mesmerizing; ten-story high, thin, vertical strips of glass alternate with vertical concrete mullions. In the winter sun the mullions are blindingly bright; even in the shade the contrast of the dark glass to white concrete is striking. Yet this minimal architecture sits here and there on highly expressive, imperfectly formed, cathedral-like vaults; in a further contradiction, these then penetrate a solid, windowless, double-story concrete form below, which stretches from one edge of the site to the other. It too is blindingly bright with sunlight. Is this a playful solid counterpart to the dissolving glass of Marina City's base?

No, surely not—for the pure solid of the single-story form itself hovers, a sheer glass plane inserted between it and the plaza's "artificial ground." The sun creates dark shadows on the surface of the recessed glass, a blackness that denies its transparency—except at the corners where the brightness and movement of State and Dearborn streets are captured through transparent glass corners. There, black-and-white abstraction melts into the chaotic color and movement of urban life.

I think to look up, and I am in awe. A dizzying perspective, framed by two circular, towering forms and a long, straight, vertical plane—residential towers and an office building—pulls me into the vast void of the sky. A moment ago I seemed to be sailing across water; now my eyes—and my body—are compelled to leap upward. I am suspended in the vertiginous blue. [Fig. 5]

A car honks—get out of the way! I remember that I have business here. Turning, I am anchored by the solid gray, lead-clad form of the theater building. It too floats on sheer glass—of the lobby floor at its base. The vertical seams of lead above seem so tactile compared to the mechanical precision of the glass below; I sense the presence of the human hand in the gentle unevenness of its surface and the rhythm of the seam cleats. I enter, back in the practical world; I walk past two extraordinary abstract paintings to an escalator that takes me down into the Marina City complex. [Fig. 6] In the distance I see a tower elevator core. People are waiting, on their way to their apartments. Will I be joining them soon?

I continue along the lobby, past restaurants, stores, many people walking. [Fig. 7] They are all soberly dressed; I feel far from the South Side. In the rental office my business begins. The rent is just beyond what I can afford, but it is close to work and I will save on travel. I know I have to live here. In the very heart of my extraordinary American, German, Polish, Italian, African American city of alleyways, railways, waterways, tunnelways, highways, airways.

The apartment to see is in Marina City's east tower. The rental agent and I walk through more sheer glass doors into the elevator lobby. The elevator doors close; my ears pop as we whoosh upwards. The agent explains that these are the fastest elevators in the city.

A surprise—first we go to the sixty-first floor—the roof deck. Exiting through the small, solid door of the circular elevator core, I stop in astonishment. In front and all around me—beyond the thin, black, steel railings at the edge—lies the breathtaking panorama of the city. After the compressed enclosure of the elevators, the endless vista is stupefying. Beneath our feet, sloping to form a shallow segment of a large sphere—my mind conjures the globe of the world—is the pale roof deck. The tall, narrow form of the elevator core continues up behind us,

→
5. Office building and residential towers, Marina City (1959–1967), Bertrand Goldberg Associates, Chicago, IL, 1964. Orlando Cabanban [photographer]. Bertrand Goldberg Archive, Ryerson and Burnham Archives, The Art Institute of Chicago. © The Art Institute of Chicago.

a white, tubular monolith. Like the deck floor, it appears glaringly bright, making this vast space feel hot, even with a chilly winter breeze on my face. I feel I could be standing on top of the world.

Unable to grasp this experience I follow the rental agent back to the elevator and we descend to the fiftieth floor. We pass through an oval tapered opening into the circular corridor serving the apartments. The corridor is dimly lit but pleasant, comforting even. The rental agent opens the apartment. Nearest to the door, she shows the compact kitchen, with sleek steel kitchen cabinets. Everything is there: stainless steel blender, toaster and mixer, even a television set. To the right I see the equally compact dressing area with mirrors from wall to wall, then the closet spaces, and bathroom; the latter sparkles with beautiful glass mosaic tiles. The bedroom beyond has floor-to-ceiling glass and a door onto half a balcony, divided from the next apartment by a metal partition—a semi-sheltered space; perfect for reading a book.

We turn back and walk out of the bedroom/bathroom suite into the living room. I gasp. In front of me I see more wall-to-wall, floor-to-ceiling glass, punctuated only by thin aluminum mullions. Beyond this glass "picture window" is the enormous curvilinear balcony; its semicircular floor and ceiling create a warm, comforting enclosure, enveloping and wrapping me even as they compel the eye beyond into the vast view they frame. Sunlight penetrates deep into the apartment, a welcome gift of midwinter warmth.

I am pulled, compelled toward the balcony. As I open the door, the sound of the city hits me. Sirens screech and cars honk above the hum of general traffic. I walk to the balcony edge; before me is the stunning urban panorama. Beyond it lies the glittering surface of Lake Michigan and in the farthest distance tiny shafts of white smoke from Michigan factories. To my right I see the other tower, a sharp silhouette against the sky. [Fig. 8] Down fifty floors flows the deep-green, ice-speckled Chicago River leading to the marina at the base of the complex.

As I lean over the balcony, above me is—once again—the endless ice-blue sky. Yet the sun warms my face and the balcony shelters me. From this beautiful, spacious, enveloping architectural opera box, I see and feel the city of Chicago in its full grandeur and life.

This is to be my first day in my Chicago home.

↖
6. Theater building and entrance to the complex, Marina City (1959–1967), Bertrand Goldberg Associates, Chicago, IL. Bertrand Goldberg Archive, Ryerson and Burnham Archives, The Art Institute of Chicago. Digital File #200203.081229-337 © The Art Institute of Chicago.

←
7. Elevator lobby, west residential tower, Marina City (1959–1967), Bertrand Goldberg Associates, Chicago, IL. Bertrand Goldberg Archive, Ryerson and Burnham Archives, The Art Institute of Chicago. © The Art Institute of Chicago.

overleaf, pp. 20–21 →
8. Balconies, Marina City (1959–1967), Bertrand Goldberg Associates, Chicago, IL, ca. 1960s. Orlando Cabanban [photographer]. Bertrand Goldberg Archive, Ryerson and Burnham Archives, The Art Institute of Chicago. Digital File #200203.081229-312 © The Art Institute of Chicago.

HUMAN DIGNITY__
A SENSE OF BELONGING
A FEELING OF IMPORTANCE
WITHIN EVERY MAN
ON EVERY JOB__
THESE MUST REMAIN
IF MEN ARE TO LIVE
AND PROSPER TOGETHER.

before marina city

YOU COULD NOT HAVE CONTEMPORARY ARCHITECTURE AS IT WAS TAUGHT AT THE BAUHAUS, AS IT WAS TAUGHT BY MIES, AS IT STILL WILL BE TAUGHT AGAIN, I AM SURE, WITHOUT A VIOLENT ECONOMIC AND A POLITICAL CHANGE. THE VALUE SYSTEM OF MODERN ARCHITECTURE CAME FROM THE VALUE SYSTEM OF POLITICAL REBELLION.

—BERTRAND GOLDBERG, *ORAL HISTORY*

Marina City was a pivotal project in Bertrand Goldberg's career. It represented the beginning of his international reputation, a significant leap in the capacity of his office, and the culmination of his previous education and professional experience. Building upon his early projects as well as his architectural training and interaction with key architects, artists, and thinkers of the twentieth century, it also intersected with architectural, socioeconomic, and cultural contexts that shaped modernist architecture and influenced Goldberg's development as an architect.

Goldberg was born in 1913 in Chicago, where he spent most of his life and died in 1997. His paternal grandparents lived in Chicago's northern suburbs, which were countryside at the time, where Goldberg's grandfather Isaac was a farmer, brick maker, and owned a general store. Goldberg's father Benjamin, one of a large family, worked in the store, and when he married Sadie Getzhof the couple moved into the city. Although the Goldbergs wanted their children to be entrepreneurs, Bertrand Goldberg's older sister Lucille Goldberg (Strauss) joined the original Goodman Theatre group in the 1920s and introduced her brother to stage design and lighting. Her theater books and stage work at Goodman were important formative experiences for her brother; however, his first career idea, at the age of twelve, was to make and publish books.[1]

Later, he studied at the Harvard School for Boys in Chicago where George Vaubel, a physics teacher, inspired him with a lifelong love for logic and "reasoning backwards."[2] His interest in intellectual inquiry led him to higher education on the East Coast and in Europe. He first studied at Harvard College and at the Cambridge School of Architecture and Landscape Architecture, the graduate architectural counterpart to Harvard College (later renamed the Graduate

←
9. Sheldon Claire exhibit wall, the Sheldon Claire Company, 520 North Michigan Avenue, Bertrand Goldberg, Chicago, IL, March 31, 1950. Hedrich-Blessing [photographer]. HB-13036-A, Chicago History Museum.

School of Design at Harvard University), then at the Bauhaus in Berlin, and finally at the Armour Institute of Technology in Chicago (now the Illinois Institute of Technology). His education at Harvard, where he discovered architecture, began in 1930; later, Dean Henry Atherton Frost allowed Goldberg, only an undergraduate student, to study architecture with him in his graduate studio.[3] He also studied with Alfred North Whitehead, a mathematician and philosopher interested in the nature of learning and liberal education. Whitehead's critique of rigid Victorian schooling led him to argue for liberal and humanist education as an amalgamation of imagination and experience, not as a mere acquisition of professional skills—ideas that resonated particularly strongly in the architecture department.[4]

Another important influence was Irving Babbitt, a scholar of romanticism in painting and literature and one of the founders of New Humanism. Goldberg was at Harvard during the Great Depression; debates with professors and fellow students centered on the social and political problems it had unleashed, and they left him with a lifelong social and political consciousness. Babbitt's emphasis on the moral imagination may have added to Goldberg's sensitivity to the ethical dimension of architecture.[5] Harvard also exposed him to the Beaux-Arts architectural tradition; he wanted to go to Paris to study this firsthand but was advised by Frost to go the Bauhaus instead.[6]

Europe and the Bauhaus
Following Frost's advice, in May 1932 at the age of nineteen, Goldberg left for Germany to attend the Bauhaus. Having moved from Dessau, the Bauhaus operated out of an abandoned telephone factory in Berlin-Steglitz but, facing increasing pressure from the National Socialist (Nazi) government, this was to be its last academic year. Larger political events accelerated this pressure. On February 27, 1933, only nine days after the last Bauhaus Ball, the Reichstag—the seat of the German parliament—burnt down; the Nazis closed the Bauhaus on April 11, 1933, and Goldberg left Berlin for Paris before catching a boat back to the United States.[7] Although he paid tuition to attend the Bauhaus, he saw its educational structure as rather loose and supplemented his education by apprenticing with Bauhaus director Ludwig Mies van der Rohe and his partner Lilly Reich. In their office, he worked under the supervision of Bruno Walter, also a Bauhaus teacher, on the design for Lemke House (1933) in Berlin.

The Bauhaus introduced him to new ideals of art and architecture. He took the introductory course and the next year's workshop courses simultaneously, finishing two academic years in one.[8] Later he wrote, "The first year's courses were largely a thing called *werklehre*. There is no good translation for *werklehre*, but it consists largely of learning how to see. *Werk* means work, and *lehre* means study—the study of how to work....You learn the world of color, you learn the world of the third dimension."[9]

The emphasis on vision and spatiality was evident in the teaching of Bauhaus faculty. Mies and Josef Albers, like the rest of the Bauhaus faculty who worked with these ideas in their teaching, left a strong mark on him. Albers, in particular, formed a close friendship with Goldberg that continued after Albers moved to the United States to teach at Black Mountain College and, later, Yale University.[10] Albers taught principles of objectivity, economy, and abstraction of form, exploring spatial compositions through the use of pure geometries to generate three-dimensional form from two-dimensional patterns—a process that Goldberg revisited in Marina City. An essential component of Albers's

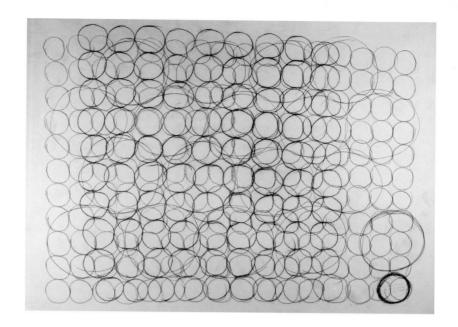

10. *Study of Circles*, Bertrand Goldberg,
Bauhaus Berlin, Germany, ca. 1932–1933.
Graphite and colored pencil on cream wove paper;
45.1 x 58.2 cm (17 3/4 x 22 15/16 in.)

three-dimensional course at the Bauhaus was the interplay of vision, color, and space.[11] Albers's "science of vision" became visible in Goldberg's Bauhaus work; one of Goldberg's many drawn studies of form, the *Study of Circles*, showed a rigorous exploration of geometry and pattern-making using repetitive circular form. [Fig. 10]

He took a variety of workship courses, including a three-dimensional course with Bruno Walter, a color class with Hinnerk Scheper, and a painting class with Wassily Kandinsky.[12] He also took a planning course with Ludwig Hilberseimer.[13] The course dealt with low-income public housing—the *Siedlungswohnungen*—and immersed Goldberg in Bauhaus ideals of service to society and industry. Goldberg was probably familiar with Hilberseimer's book *Grosstadt Architektur* (1927) and his Project for a Skyscraper City (unbuilt, 1924), both of which presented an industrial vision of the city. Project for a Skyscraper City—comprising large slab blocks resting on solid platforms—was similar in some ways to Marina City.

The Bauhaus had an active social life. Goldberg designed invitations for the last Bauhaus Festival held February 18, 1933. The circular format, sans serif typeface, and minimal layout echoed his student work. At the Bauhaus he also had many American and German friends; however, one of his most significant encounters was with Russian Menshevik economist and émigré Vladimir Woytinsky, a commissar on the western front during the Menshevik Revolution and later chief statistician for German trade unions.[14] Woytinsky wanted to come to the United States (and later did), and so he met with Goldberg to practice English. Goldberg in turn learned about socialism and economics from Woytinsky and helped translate Woytinsky's book on revolutionary activity.[15] Through their conversations Goldberg also learned to bridge political and aesthetic activity and to span social and professional boundaries. [Fig. 11]

The Bauhaus period also initiated his interest in "a value system that was based on industry."[16] For him this Bauhaus credo contrasted sharply with architectural modernism in the United States, which was centered on style; he felt that it missed important ideas about contemporary society and industrial production. He later wrote:

fest
im bauhaus
kostümfest im künstler-kreise
sonnabend
18. februar 21ʰ
in den räumen des
bauhauses
berlin-steglitz, birkbuschstrasse 55/56
telefon: g 9 albrecht 5808 und 2165

11. Bauhaus Festival invitation
(front face), Bertrand Goldberg, Bauhaus
Berlin, Germany, February 18, 1933.

the Bauhaus was striving to extinguish—the concept of style, of applied style. Architecture, art, painting, photography, dance, theater, literature was supposed to emerge naturally out of a society which was recognized as an industrialized society.[17]

He also criticized the architecture of Le Corbusier, who was perceived at the Bauhaus as a painter and stylist but not necessarily an activist architect:[18]

A quotation from one of Corbusier's books has stuck in my mind all my life—that the right angle was the perfect form because with it you could measure everything....It was in the fifties that I realized that there was such a thing as a Right Angle Society, and that it had a historical tradition that certainly came out of the late nineteenth century....Corbu was not an anthropologist or he would have been more aware of the fact that there are societies where there are no words for the right angle; where the concept of a right angle doesn't exist.[19]

The rejection of the right angle would reach new heights in his professional work on Marina City.

His relationship to Mies was more complex—involving both fascination and distance. Their association continued after they reunited in Chicago in the late 1930s, with Goldberg even calling Mies his "father."[20] Mies used to visit his office, look at his designs, and provide critiques and was reported to have said that he "was among the most imaginative of his students."[21] A careful student of Mies's work, he was impressed with his teacher's precision and attention to detail, asking, "Why did Mies turn this corner? In which way did he move his spaces from one place to another—from indoors to outdoors, from outdoors to indoors, from one room to another?"[22]

Another important Bauhaus lesson was Mies's and Albers's design process based on repetition and iteration. Goldberg welcomed its disciplined exploration:

Mies, I think, was very helpful in giving me an understanding of the enormous discipline that any creative work requires. Albers similarly, with the working over and over and over—the refinement, the wringing out of ideas, the throwing away. As someone said in literature, any time you think you've written a good paragraph, throw it away, tear up your paper. The same thing applies, really, in architecture. Any time you think you have a great design, throw it away.[23]

His later professional career drew on these beginnings; a project of Marina City's complexity required endless iterations and negotiations, and built on lessons begun at the Bauhaus. He later said: "Architecturally speaking, I never parted ways with Mies....The discipline of taking a total design and out of that totality working out the details, the discipline of creating an aesthetic out of the structure, the discipline of seeking an alliance with an industrial world, that discipline I still have."[24]

Mies's professional work formed another influence—his glass skyscraper designs of the 1920s anticipated the complex geometries of Marina City. Although never built, these projects were widely published, contributing to Mies's stature as a pioneer of modernist architecture. Architectural historians had, Goldberg believed, underestimated the importance of this work.[25] His philosophy education also allowed him to contextualize Mies's "less is more" within the Middle Ages, a period Goldberg admired.[26] Yet he criticized Mies for the same reason he dismissed Le Corbusier, for fetishizing the right angle:

> We have just left the Victorian period in architectural and engineering concepts…Gropius, Corbusier (until 1950), and Mies van der Rohe, these men were the romanticists who made of the right angle a cult and who refined the expressions of the right angle architecturally into a creed. Our time has made us aware that forces and strains flow in patterns which have little relationship to the rectilinear concepts of the Victorian engineer.[27]

Marina City would break away from the "Victorian right angle"—a departure in Goldberg's work from raw Bauhaus ideals to a more developed individual approach and a merger of Bauhaus principles with the socioeconomic impact of the Great Depression and the architecture of the Midwest.

Chicago Apprenticeships

In 1933 Goldberg returned to Chicago to study structural engineering at the Armour Institute of Technology. He worked as an apprentice to his professors—to ensure his German engineering knowledge translated to Chicago, to broaden his engineering vocabulary, and to prepare for the professional licensing exam. At the Armour Institute he took classes in structural engineering from Frank Nydam, who later would provide engineering support for Goldberg's office. In 1935, following a recommendation by the architect Philip Johnson, Goldberg apprenticed with George Fred Keck, known as Fred. The firm Keck and Keck, founded in 1926 by Keck, included his brother William Keck as well as other architects and apprentices; many would later become significant architects and educators.[28] Fred Keck was one of the pioneers of Midwest architectural modernism and industrialized building. His House of Tomorrow (1933) and Crystal House (1934) were built for A Century of Progress International Exposition, the 1933–34 World's Fair in Chicago. The exhibition, an amalgamation of technological inventions funded by both private and state capital, envisioned a future based on scientific progress. Keck and Keck's House of Tomorrow had a radial polygonal plan with a central tubular core as a primary structural element, a rudimentary form of air-conditioning, and large glass windows incorporated into its passive solar heating system—formal and environmental principles similar to Goldberg's later explorations in Marina City. [Fig. 12] Keck's interest in Goldberg's Bauhaus experience was not a coincidence—he brought László Moholy-Nagy to Chicago, later teaching at the New Bauhaus and then chairing the Department of Architecture at the Institute of Design. At Keck and Keck Goldberg explored architectural prefabrication and building technology, including mechanical systems in modern housing. Keck and Keck's commercial housing foreshadowed Goldberg's later residential projects in Chicago and its suburbs.

Keck and Keck's office was also an important meeting place for progressive architects. While there Goldberg met Leland Atwood (son of Charles B. Atwood of Burnham and Atwood), the principal draftsman who had also worked for the architects R. Buckminster Fuller and David Adler; in the 1950s Atwood would briefly become Goldberg's business partner. Goldberg also met Fuller, an important influence, through the avant-garde Chicago painter Rudolph

**12. House of Tomorrow at the Chicago
Century of Progress International
Exposition, George Fred Keck and
William Keck, Chicago, IL, 1933.**
Hedrich-Blessing [photographer]. HB-27620,
Chicago History Museum.

Weisenborn. Like Goldberg, Fuller was a person of varied interests—designing vehicles, houses, and communities, and working as a researcher, engineer, architect, and product designer. In 1936 Goldberg designed a rear-engine car, whose aerodynamic form was clearly inspired by Fuller's three-wheeled Dymaxion Car (1933) presented at the Century of Progress exhibition.

In the mid-1930s Goldberg also worked for Howard T. Fisher, a registered architect, an engineer, and a cartographer. His firm, General Housing, founded in 1932, pioneered U.S. prefabricated housing; there Goldberg learned about the integration of design, manufacturing, cost estimating, and marketing in design.[29] Fisher's General House, which cost $4,500 to purchase and was designed and built for the 1933 Century of Progress exhibition, was made of metal panels coated with enamel porcelain.[30] For Goldberg this formed an important example of residential prefabrication.[31]

Another important Chicago architect for whom he worked was Robert Paul Schweikher, whose work was included in the landmark exhibition Modern Architecture: International Exhibition (1932) at the Museum of Modern Art in New York City. At Schweikher's firm Schweikher and Elting, Goldberg learned the practical business of running an office and was exposed to the ideas of Frank Lloyd Wright and the Prairie School.[32] These influences were particularly evident in Schweikher's home and studio in suburban Chicago (1937). Mainly brick and wood, its horizontal planes and cantilevered volumes were rooted in the principles of Wright's Usonian House. Although such materials lay beyond Goldberg's vision of industrialized form, Usonian principles resonated with the Bauhaus's and Fisher's ideas of affordable housing.[33] At Schweikher's office Goldberg may also have encountered Wright's concrete "mushroom" columns in the S. C. Johnson and Son Administration Building (1936), now known as the Johnson Wax Building—a possible influence on the sculptural concrete columns in Marina City.

If Wright possibly provided structural inspiration, architect Louis Sullivan definitely provided programmatic influences on Goldberg's work. Sullivan's Auditorium Building (1889) in Chicago formed an important precedent for Marina City as an urban mixed-use complex, integrating offices, a hotel, and a theater in a single development. Although he makes little reference to Sullivan in his Oral History, they met when Goldberg was only twelve years old, having watched people on the stairs of the Auditorium Building, fascinated by the connection of its public spaces with its mixed-use program.[34] In a way, Marina City is an exoskeletal version of the Auditorium Building—a variation of Sullivan's building turned inside out. Goldberg was also a careful reader of Sullivan's texts. In 1986, he used the title of Sullivan's famous series of essays "Kindergarten Chats" as a basis for his own essay about Mies—"Kindergarten Plauderei" (Kindergarten chats).[35]

Early Practice

In 1937 Goldberg formed an independent practice in his own name. He worked alone until the start of World War II, mainly on residential projects. He focused on getting his office off the ground, but he also nurtured his Bauhaus contacts. In December 1938, his name was listed as one of the contributors to PLUS: Orientations of Contemporary Architecture, a special bimonthly supplement to Architectural Forum magazine.[36] Commissioned by Forum's editor Howard Myers, PLUS featured modernist graphic design by Herbert Matter. Its contributors included artists Albers and Moholy-Nagy; architects Marcel Breuer, Fisher,

13. North Pole Mobile Ice Cream Store, Bertrand Goldberg, Gilmer V. Black, River Forest, IL, 1938. Hedrich-Blessing [photographer]. HB-4878-A, Chicago History Museum.

Fuller, Richard Neutra, Schweikher, Fred Keck, and Le Corbusier; architectural historian Siegfried Giedion, sculptor Naum Gabo, and others. *PLUS* documented international case studies in modernist design as an effort to promote it in the United States. It was in this context of emerging U.S. modernism that Goldberg developed his own practice.

His first independent commission was in 1934 for a house for Harriet Higginson, an early feminist according to him.[37] He was attentive to his first client's needs—Higginson wanted an easily maintained structure, washable by a garden hose.[38] These desires matched his interest in prefabrication, resulting in a simple single-room house. Building it as a wood frame structure, with wood sheathing covered with canvas, similar to that used on aircraft, made it more affordable; it cost only $1,200 and a solar heating system helped with further savings.[39]

In 1938 he designed another prefabricated structure—the North Pole Mobile Ice Cream Store in Chicago. [Fig. 13] Inspired by Fuller's Dymaxion House (1929) and Keck and Keck's House of Tomorrow, the store had transparent glass walls and a cantilevered tension-cable supported roof, similar to a sailboat mast. The mast was anchored to a truck trailer whose chassis formed part of the building, making the entire structure portable.[40] Around this mast an open, airy, and transparent space emerged—a concept that would resurface in Marina City. The North Pole Mobile Ice Cream Store also anticipated Marina City's entrepreneurial ideas in that he tried to sell the concept to the Sears, Roebuck and Company, albeit without success. However, a different and lifelong collaboration emerged. Hedrich-Blessing, a Chicago architectural photography practice just emerging in the 1930s but soon to become the photographer of choice for its modernist architects, photographed the North Pole project. Hedrich-Blessing's nighttime photograph embodied the firm's signature-style—high contrast with an emphasis on light and shadow, and lightness and transparency of materials. The photographers of Hedrich-Blessing would become Goldberg's favorites.

Finance and management of prefabricated housing, which often involved partnerships between public and private funders, became another strong interest for him. In late 1930s he and his then associate, architect Gilmer Black, with partners Edwin "Squirrel" Ashcroft (an attorney) and Ross Beatty (the landowner), started a cooperative called the Standard Houses Corporation. Its aim was to build an affordable prefabricated home they called the Standard House.

The first house was built in 1937 for Purdue University's Housing Research Project in Lafayette, Indiana. Goldberg made a separate drawing of each piece of wood to be used in the house to fully understand its assembly. Five more homes were built as a small development in Melrose Park, Illinois, between 1939 and 1941. These single-story, gabled-roofed houses each had two bedrooms, a bathroom, a kitchen, and a living room, with attic storage space. Goldberg and his partners acted as developers: Beatty gave the land for the development, and each partner contributed one hundred dollars toward the building cost. The team also marketed the houses, selling all in a single day for only $2,995 each.[41]

In an attempt to collaborate with the construction industry, Goldberg traveled to New York City to meet with the president of the newly formed US Plywood Corporation to convince him to give the team credit to buy plywood and other lumber used in the project.[42] In addition, Goldberg arranged three meetings with the Federal Housing Administration (FHA) in Washington, D.C., convincing it to insure the project's mortgages—experience that would later contribute to Marina City's viability.[43] In 1942 this work led to a government contract for the design and construction of an entire community—the new town of Suitland, Maryland. In this project Goldberg developed experience in construction and project management, from site planning to delivery, and collaborated with architect Eero Saarinen, who did government-sponsored color studies for the houses.[44]

Work on prefabrication exposed Goldberg to the relationship between labor unions and industrial building production. Historically, unions had resisted industrialization, fearing its impact on the building industry's demand for labor. He found ways to build prefabricated houses with union agreements, including agreements with the American Federation of Labor (AFL):

> We designed our production methods with various union agreements— with the carpenters unions, with the plumbers union. We had the first union agreements and the only union agreements in the country. Every other prefabricated house was built non-union. We built with union labor....We unionized our factory.[45]

Moving "from the artisanship of building to industrialized production," he became an engineer and contract manager: "We set up production lines the way you build an automobile. We had conveyors and we had men doing one operation and not another and becoming proficient in doing just one operation."[46] This Fordist approach to construction was according to Goldberg a legacy of the Great Depression that forced union workers to accept dramatic changes in work practices to keep their jobs.[47]

The public also accepted his designs, but for another reason: price. After Melrose Park he realized that affordability made progressive design ideas acceptable. He observed, "If one is too radical, the comfort level decreases and has to be compensated for in some other way, for example, in cost. If you build something inexpensively enough, people will buy it no matter whether they approve of your style or not because they buy for economic reasons."[48]

He also had a keen interest in industrial design. During World War II he designed antiaircraft gun crates that converted into living quarters. He also designed, manufactured, and distributed a standard prefabricated bathroom, installed with only four connections: hot and cold water, drainage, and ventilation. He fondly called it Unican (1946). [Fig. 14] Unican contained a bathtub, a shower, a sink, and a toilet and cost only $275 to $375, including installation.[49] He also designed a special marketing brochure, an early use of printed publicity, which would reach its peak with Marina City.

His interest in industrial design was also evident in his design of a prefabricated freight car that he called Unicel (1950–1952). [Fig. 15] Designed in response to the postwar shortage of steel, its stressed plywood tubular form was, in his words, a "brick" of space.[50] It foreshadowed Marina City's vertical core system—Unicel flipped vertically. Here too he was actively involved in Unicel's marketing, producing printed brochures and full-scale mock-ups to convince skeptics that plywood was structurally sound and the cars were functionally feasible. However, the steel industry lobby fought the project and despite initial approval by the Technical Committee of the Association of American Railroads, the project collapsed amid concerns of its deadly impact on the American steel industry. Nevertheless, Unicel helped advance Goldberg's marketing abilities, with the Unicel mock-up installation in particular anticipating Marina City's apartment mock-ups. Building on the marketing expertise developed for Unican, the project and its glamorous printed materials were introduced at gala events in Chicago and at the Waldorf-Astoria Hotel in New York City. Unicel reached a new apogee in Unishelter (1953), a self-contained mobile housing development using the same stressed-skin plywood as Unicel. Here too he orchestrated the production of printed marketing materials.

His work with full-scale mock-ups also included his exhibition design for Sheldon-Claire Company, a Chicago advertising agency producing motivational posters for industry. The exhibition, Exhibits from Sheldon-Claire Employee Education Program, included images of the human body suspended between quotations and mechanical drawings, presenting a harmonious relationship between industrial production, humanity, and progress, so embodying principles advocated by not only Sheldon-Claire Company but also by Goldberg himself (see Fig. 9).

In 1952 he completed the Snyder House on Shelter Island, New York, an important prefabricated house that defined his mature industrial aesthetic. [Fig. 16] The house was designed for John Snyder, the chairman-president of the Pressed Steel Car Company, which was to manufacture the steel components of Unicel boxcars and Unishelter houses. An elongated stressed plywood tube, the house used the same material, structural, and manufacturing logic as its precedents. Including a bathroom, a kitchen, plumbing, and a heating, ventilation, and

DESIGNED FOR MAXIMUM LIVING
DESIGNED FOR MINIMUM CARE

CHECK
ALL THESE
MODERN FEATURES

✓ WATER TIGHT WALL PROTECTORS
✓ FLUSH EASY-TO-CLEAN CONSTRUCTION
✓ CONTINUOUS RECESSED TOE-SPACE
✓ BUILT-IN-MEDICINE CABINET
✓ BUILT-IN-LINEN CABINET
✓ MAGAZINE RACK AND ASH TRAY
✓ ALL PIPES EASILY ACCESSIBLE

FOR MOTHERS....

EASY
TO
CLEAN
(AND
KEEP
CLEAN)

**14. "Bathroom Building Comes of Age,"
brochure, p. 1, Standard Fabrication Inc.,
Bertrand Goldberg, Chicago, IL, ca. 1946.**
Photograph. Bertrand Goldberg Archive, Ryerson
and Burnham Archives, The Art Institute of Chicago.
© The Art Institute of Chicago.

**15. Unicel Prefabricated Box Car,
Pressed Steel Car Company, Bertrand
Goldberg, Chicago, IL, ca. 1950–1951.**
Photograph. Bertrand Goldberg Archive, Ryerson
and Burnham Archives, The Art Institute of Chicago.
© The Art Institute of Chicago.

**16. John Snyder Residence, Bertrand
Goldberg, Shelter Island, NY, 1952.**
Photograph. Bertrand Goldberg Archive, Ryerson
and Burnham Archives, The Art Institute of Chicago.
© The Art Institute of Chicago.

air-conditioning (HVAC) system, it was made in Chicago and shipped for assembly on-site. Its dramatic cantilever loomed over the water's edge, highlighting the lightness and aerodynamic form possible with prefabricated structures. The plywood elements were made of naturally finished mahogany plywood. The stark modernism of the exterior was countered by an interior featuring a massive stone fireplace and flagstone floors, in strong contrast to the glass, steel, and plywood of the exterior. Bauhaus-, Keck and Keck-, and Fisher-inspired industrial production met Schweikher's Prairie-style modernism, making the Snyder House a true synthesis of Goldberg's training and professional practice to date.

Bertrand Goldberg Associates

The end of World War II provided new opportunities for Goldberg's practice. During the war he had been assisted by Bill Ahern, a building contractor-engineer. Now his other collaborators included Bill Priestley, an architect and fellow Bauhaus student; Bill Fyfe, a Yale-trained architect who had worked for Schweikher; and Ralph Bernardini, who worked as the model maker and held a professional engineering license. From 1950 to 1952 Goldberg partnered with Leland Atwood to form Goldberg and Atwood, Architects and Engineers, until Atwood returned to work for Buckminster Fuller. His other associates at the time included Gilmer Black as draftsman, Frank Nydam as structural engineer, and Alfred Caldwell as landscape consultant. In 1954, some time after Atwood left, the office was incorporated as Bertrand Goldberg Associates (BGA) and by the time of Marina City's commission in 1959 there were eight to ten people in the office.[51]

In the postwar period Goldberg's professional life also intersected with his private life. In 1946, he married his second wife, Nancy Florsheim, daughter of Lillian and Irving Florsheim of the Florsheim Shoe Company.[52] Lillian Florsheim, his mother-in-law, was an accomplished artist and art collector. She had studied with the painter Hugo Weber and was close to the abstract sculptor and painter Georges Vantongerloo, cofounder of the de Stijl movement. Later Denise René, Florsheim's close friend and owner of an important modern art gallery in Paris, steered Lillian toward Naum Gabo's dynamic forms and modern materials. Florsheim's extensive art collection centered on the relationship between geometry and three-dimensional form using translucent materials, and it included works by Vantongerloo and Gabo. Her own artwork investigated two- and three-dimensional abstract form and geometric pattern. She experimented with linear and circular themes, often working in Lucite, a type of Plexiglas. Some of her work paralleled Goldberg's, including his early Lucite model of Marina City discussed in the next chapter.

She also briefly became her son-in-law's patron. In 1952 he designed her kitchen, a small project forming a bridge between two houses—both a corridor and a kitchen. The kitchen had an island on each side with built-in cabinets and curved stainless steel "garages" with roll-up doors—convenient storage spaces for electrical kitchen appliances. An important feature was a curved fiberglass wall—the same material that would later be used as formwork for the Marina City residential towers and office building vault structure.

Curvilinear Form

In the mid-1950s Goldberg designed a rectilinear garage structure, only to realize the differential structural load on columns in different locations—those at the

edges carried lower loads than those in the middle. He recognized that the rectilinear mass-production aesthetic so vigorously promulgated by his Bauhaus teachers was neither efficient nor reproducible as it involved a number of custom-made corner pieces. That discovery led him to reinvestigate tubular forms; these evolved into a series of projects culminating in the Marina City design.

His early exploration of curved concrete form was particularly evident in two projects completed in 1957—the City of Nashville Sewage Plant and the Pineda Island Recreation Center in Mobile, Alabama. Designed to manage the collection and treatment of the entire sewage system of the City of Nashville, the Sewage Plant explored the structural possibilities of curvilinear concrete forms—including the way that formwork was made and placed. The Pineda Island Recreation Center made extensive use of circular and organic forms in plan and within individual structural elements, and it most likely used fiberglass formwork that later resurfaced in Marina City. [Fig. 17]

He also designed Motel 66 (unbuilt, 1957) for a Chicago South Side site. [Fig. 18] Commissioned by the Phillips Petroleum Company, the project included twin circular towers positioned on a rectangular base, similar to the Marina City massing. The towers' facades had a gridded louver system anticipating the Astor Tower project (1961–1963).

His experiments with circular form paralleled the work of other architects. An important precedent was Buckminster Fuller's four-dimensional tower (1928, unbuilt), featuring a prominent central circular core with cantilevered floor plates; it anticipated the form and logic of Marina City in its diagrams demonstrating aerodynamic advantages of circular form. He knew Fuller and would have known of the project itself through Leland Atwood, who had worked on the tower's sketches.[53] In 1949 I. M. Pei designed a round residential tower with apartments rising in a helical pattern.[54] Though Goldberg was aware of this project, he denied its influence, stating that unlike Marina City's tubular form, Pei's design was a helical post-and-beam system.[55] Nevertheless, Pei's project questioned the primacy of rectilinear form as the only legitimate expression of structural, functional, and urban logic. Farther afield, Pier Luigi Nervi in his ferroconcrete work of the late 1950s used structural and constructional logic to question rectilinear geometries. Goldberg admired Nervi's work, not only for its design but also for Nervi's ability to deliver design, engineering, and installation in a single package such as the Palazzetto dello Sport (1958) in Rome. In his *Oral History* Goldberg also mentioned South American architects—presumably referring to Oscar Niemeyer's curvilinear and circular concrete structures in Brazil.

Circular forms and prefabricated formwork had great engineering and architectural advantage, allowing structures to be erected in record time.[56] Although he did not cite the works of architects Eduardo Torroja, Félix Candela, or Giovanni Michelucci, they all built curvilinear concrete structures before Marina City. Torroja's work preceded it by two decades. Michelucci's vertical city project for San Remo (unbuilt, 1950–1952) featured twin towers linked by bridges—as Goldberg was to propose in residential projects after Marina City. Goldberg also made no reference to architect Louis Kahn's National Assembly Building (1961–1982) in Dhaka, Bangladesh, which explored circular form similar to Marina City. Although its construction began, two years later than that of Marina City, Kahn had explored circular form earlier in his Civic Center proposal (unbuilt, 1956–1957) for Philadelphia, with circular parking structures acting as gateways to a downtown "forum."

Rectangular Form

Nevertheless, rectilinear form continued to be an important focus of Goldberg's projects in the 1950s. In two housing projects—Northree Apartments (unbuilt, 1952) for Kansas City, Missouri, and the Drexel Boulevard Town and Garden Apartments (1953–1957) in Chicago—he responded to the postwar housing boom. Northree Apartments won a national competition sponsored by *Progressive Architecture*. Their cruciform shape with an open central core containing stairs and elevators, as well as their planning and use of concrete, can be seen as a precedent for Marina City. The Drexel Boulevard Town and Garden Apartments were completed for one of the most influential Chicago developers of the time—Arthur Rubloff. [Fig. 19] Built with floor-to-ceiling transparent and opaque glass facades facing the street and back patios, the floor structure consisted of concrete beams and precast concrete planking. This was not true public housing—the project typified private-public collaboration in which a private developer built affordable housing for the city. Goldberg partnered with Rubloff because he believed that government funding was not sufficient to design dignified affordable homes. Sold for fifteen thousand dollars, each three-bedroom townhouse was priced competitively with its public counterpart and came fully equipped with kitchen, laundry, heating, and air conditioning.[57] As in Marina City later, tenants had full control of their utility supplies, reducing the central management associated with the inefficiency of pubic housing. One of the project's goals was to integrate African Americans and Caucasians, but, despite its siting in a traditionally African American neighborhood, private lenders would not provide loans to African Americans.[58] Reality tempered ideals, so the developer and architect had to compromise and build only for Caucasian residents.

The design for the Universal Recording Corporation (1958) in Chicago foreshadowed the design of Marina City's commercial platform. [Fig. 20] Topped by a penthouse and penetrated by a grid of columns, the horizontal glazed first-floor volume of this two-story structure cantilevered over its base in a formal composition resembling Marina City's restaurant hovering over the marina.

At the time BGA was beginning to work on Marina City, it was also working on Astor Tower. [Fig. 21] Conceived before Marina City, Astor Tower's construction was delayed and it was completed in 1963 shortly before the residential component of Marina City opened. Designed as an executive-type business hotel, it has a square concrete core with stairs and two elevators surrounded by four one-bedroom apartments. The apartments are relatively small and can be combined to form larger units. The structural system anticipated that of Marina City—the slip form system rose up to make the central concrete core surrounded by a beam system supporting the floors. The round tubular columns are exposed both outside and inside. The core resists about 90 percent of the wind stress, an important structural feature repeated in Marina City.[59] The typical floor plan starts on the fifth floor, with concrete core and exterior columns fully visible below. This gives the building a particularly elongated and elegant appearance, crowned by the extended core rising above the line of the roof deck, which, as at Marina City, covers the entire footprint of the building and can be used as a skating rink. The decision to raise the main volume of the building was virtue born of necessity: the zoning code limited the square footage on-site. Since the lot size did not leave enough room for the car ramp leading to the parking below, a large car elevator was also installed. Such vertical mobility would be revisited in studies of boat elevators in the marina for Marina City. Another important feature of Astor Tower were its exterior louvers—later removed during

**19. Drexel Town and Garden Apartments
(1953–54), Bertrand Goldberg
Associates, Chicago, IL.** Hedrich-Blessing
[photographer]. HB-27871, Bertrand Goldberg Archive,
Ryerson and Burnham Archives, The Art Institute of
Chicago. Courtesy of The Art Institute of Chicago
© The Chicago History Museum

20. Walton Gardens, Universal Recording Corporation Building, Bertrand Goldberg Associates, Chicago, IL, ca. 1955. Bertrand Goldberg Archive, Ryerson and Burnham Archives, The Art Institute of Chicago. Digital File #200203.081229-600 © The Art Institute of Chicago.

21. Astor Tower, Bertrand Goldberg Associates, Chicago, IL, 1961. Bertrand Goldberg Archive, Ryerson and Burnham Archives, The Art Institute of Chicago. Digital File #200203.081229-030 © The Art Institute of Chicago.

renovation—which were controlled from within each unit to provide protection from weather and dirt. The interior windows were fully detachable and could be taken down and washed in the underground garage. The ever-changing pattern of light and shadow created by the louvers animated the entire facade; this play of light, both during day and night, would emerge as a recurring theme in Goldberg's work, including at Marina City.

An important project leading up to Marina City was the Helstein House (1950–1956) in Chicago. It was originally intended to be a complex set of steel volumes, only to be completely redesigned and built with concrete pilotis and floor slabs resembling Le Corbusier's design for Maison Dom-ino (unbuilt, 1914). The facade was pulled back, however, fully exposing the concrete structure, with glass walls and steel mullions receding into the background. It was supported by round monolithic concrete columns cast using spiral cardboard tubes as formwork. Traces of these were clearly visible in Hedrich-Blessing's photographs of the house. A dramatic suspended staircase linked the carport and small foyer on the ground floor to the second-floor open-plan living and dining area, kitchen, and three bedrooms. The client, Ralph Helstein, was the president of the United Packinghouse, Food and Allied Workers, an activist in the civil rights movement, and a close friend of Martin Luther King Jr.; he was also an intellectual and a teacher.[60]

Finally, collaborating with Leland Atwood, Goldberg designed a low-budget structure (1950) for the International Union of Operating Engineers (IUOE) Local 399 on Jackson Street, including an auditorium and a display space for products made by union members and featuring thermopane windows and reinforced concrete. It is likely that Helstein or the president of the IUOE introduced Goldberg to William McFetridge, president of the Building Services Employees International Union (also known as the Janitors' Union), when McFetridge was looking for an architect to remodel his organization's offices at 318 West Randoph Street. Although his redesign for the union's Chicago headquarters was modest, its impact on his practice was profound: it connected him to the labor leader who would soon commission Marina City.

22. Bertrand Goldberg, William
McFetridge, and Charles Swibel with
the Marina City model. Hedrich-Blessing
[photographer]. HB-23215-F, Chicago History Museum.

chapter two

unpacking marina city

THE THEATER, THE RESTAURANTS, THE OFFICES, THE PARK-
ING, THE RETAIL, THE RECREATIONAL, THE BOATING AND,
OF COURSE, THE APARTMENTS — ALL WERE BOUND UP AND
DEPENDED UPON EACH OTHER FOR A SUCCESSFUL LIVING
CHEEK BY JOWL.

—BERTRAND GOLDBERG, *ORAL HISTORY*

Though we often think of Marina City exclusively in terms of its corncob-shaped twin towers, it is actually a complex of five structures—two residential towers, a rectangular office building, a saddle-shaped theater building, and a commercial platform on which all the other structures stand. The complex was commissioned by the Building Service Employees International Union, later renamed the Service Employees International Union and in this book simply referred to as the Janitors' Union. It provided a powerful urban vision, promoting the social and economic need of urban blue-collar workers to live and "play" near their workplace. At a time of "white flight" to the suburbs it also fueled Mayor Richard J. Daley's plan to revitalize downtown Chicago—the first, and, for a long time, the only downtown residential mixed-use complex and a prophetic model for Chicago's future downtown revival.

Marina City emerged from the confluence of three worlds: those of Bertrand Goldberg, the architect and sole principal of Bertrand Goldberg Associates; William McFetridge, the project client and president of the Building Service Employees International Union (the Janitors' Union); and Charles "Chuck" Swibel, the project developer and president of Marks and Company, a Chicago real estate firm. Their vision, experience, money, and influence permanently changed Chicago and federal rules defining urban development and housing finance. Together with other key national and regional political and financial figures, these three men drove the Marina City proposal from initial planning and financial discussions to the final design, construction, and letting of the complex.

His role extending beyond the drafting board, Goldberg not only gave Marina City its form, spatial organization, and urban purpose but also helped advance the team's financial, political, and urban ambitions, symbolizing its "capitalism for the common man." He came to the project with the belief—seasoned in the Depression, European interwar turmoil, and World War II—that architecture within a capitalist democracy must embrace industry and equality. Recognizing his limited experience in housing and none at the scale of Marina City, he observed: "My background was totally different, but they loved my ideas. They were amused by my innocence to a great extent, and they respected my work. In a measure, it was a perfect combination to build Marina City."[1]

At the time McFetridge was nearly seventy years old, in his nineteenth year as the Janitors' Union president. A prominent figure in the American Federation of Labor-Congress of Industrial Organizations (AFL-CIO) to which the Janitors' Union belonged, Goldberg called him "a great man, brilliant and sophisticated, and yet publicly he was a labor stiff; he was corrupt in many ways as the labor movement was corrupt.... [But] he understood that he had a responsibility beyond being simply a labor stiff."[2] The Janitors' Union had begun as Chicago Flat Janitors' Union Local 14332 in 1912. It joined other small janitors' unions in 1921 to become the Building Service Employees International Union (BSEIU) and then, in 1968, became Service Employees International Union (SEIU), which is its current title.[3] Joining it as the nephew of its founding president William Quesse, McFetridge quickly rose through the ranks. In 1937 he lost the union's presidency to George Scalise, elected in large part due to his mob connections. In 1940, after Scalise's conviction for labor racketeering, embezzlement, and bribery, he became the Janitors' Union's president and began to distance it from organized crime. During his twenty-year presidency he expanded its membership from 40,000 to 250,000 members. A Catholic and close confidante of Mayor Richard J. Daley, McFetridge conominated Daley for his 1954 mayoral bid, which led to Daley's seventeen-year reign as "America's Pharaoh."[4]

Trade unions of the period were deeply enmeshed within state and federal politics and McFetridge's organization was no exception. As vice-president of the Illinois State Federation of Labor, McFetridge was a powerful force in the national and international labor movement. He was instrumental in the merger of the AFL with the Congress of Industrial Organizations (CIO) and became its vice-president and a member of its executive council in 1950. He served on the federal Legislative and Political Education, Civil Rights, Housing and Veterans' Affairs committees and was active in the international political arena. In Chicago, McFetridge was vice-president, among others, of the Board of Commissioners of the Chicago Park District and the Illinois Public Building Commission, and he was involved in cross-denominational philanthropy.[5] Yet as Marina City was becoming a reality, he voluntarily stepped down from the Janitors' Union's presidency, giving his support to his long-time protégé David Sullivan, president of the Janitors' Union Local 32B in New York, who in 1960 became the Janitors' Union's president. Almost immediately after his election, Sullivan distanced himself from his mentor, prompting McFetridge to reverse course and attempt reelection as president. A bitter battle for the Janitors' Union's leadership began and Marina City became one of the battlegrounds, as will be seen later.[6]

Swibel, the developer, and the Janitors' Union's realtor was allegedly the "mastermind behind the financing of Marina City."[7] Only thirty-five years old at the time of Marina City's groundbreaking, Swibel—born Shaia Rchaim Cwibel—was a poster-child for the American dream.[8] The son of a Polish-born

→
23. View of the complex from River North, Marina City (1959–1967), Bertrand Goldberg Associates, Chicago, IL. Hedrich-Blessing [photographer]. HB-23215-H5, Chicago History Museum.

bootmaker, within five years of his arrival in the United States he was an honor high school student and then a premedical scholarship student at the University of Illinois.[9] He worked at Marks and Company while still a student, when its president Isaac Marks offered to pay for his tuition and books and raise his pay if Swibel took courses in commerce and finance at Northwestern University. "That determined my fate," Swibel said. "It was the difference between poverty and riches for my family."[10]

Swibel too entered the Chicago political machine early. He met McFetridge on a trip to Israel and shortly afterwards Marks and Company became the real estate agents for the Janitors' Union. In 1956 Richard J. Daley appointed Swibel, who was only twenty-nine years old, as commissioner and treasurer of the Chicago Housing Authority (CHA), an appointment apparently engineered by McFetridge so that Swibel would represent union interests.[11] The Chicago press, acknowledging the poor reputation of Marks and Company, proclaimed, "Daley Gives Post to Skid Row Agent."[12] Swibel became president of Marks and Company in 1959 on Isaac Marks's death. Only three years later he became president of the Marina City Management Corporation and vice-chairman of the CHA. He became CHA's chairman in 1964, an appointment that was to be troubled. Goldberg was aware of Swibel's strengths and shortcomings, stating that Swibel "understood more about other people's greed, perhaps, than McFetridge understood. Swibel had no illusions and he, in a sense, did the things that other people wanted to have done for them but wouldn't do themselves."[13] Swibel, like McFetridge, was involved in cross-denominational interests. He was a board member of Auxiliary Archbishop Bernard. J. Sheil's foundation and co-chairman of Chicago's State of Israel bond drive.[14] Sheil, in a partisan *Chicago Daily News* article, described Swibel as having a "tremendous concern for the poor. He has a great heart, a heart that feels."[15]

If McFetridge's motivation in building Marina City was primarily political, Swibel's was mainly financial. He proudly boasted in 1961, "It's been the stimulus, I think, for half a billion dollars worth of building in the Loop. Now I want to pay off the mortgage and call it my own. And I will…then I'll be a millionaire."[16] Yet he also believed in the project's progressive urban vision, stating, "I'd love to be among the first to find the formula for young people just married. The ideal place in the city. Because then I would prove all the experts wrong about the exodus to the suburbs."[17] And it was his wife, Seena, who apparently came up with the Marina City name.[18] [Fig. 23]

The Idea

In a casual conversation in the late 1950s Swibel and McFetridge agreed that McFetridge should follow the example of some New York unions and invest health, welfare, and pension funds in low-cost housing.[19] U.S. trade unions had sponsored housing already in the 1920s, when Abraham E. Kazan, the president of the Amalgamated Clothing Workers Credit Union, spearheaded the construction of the Amalgamated Cooperative Apartment House project in the Bronx. Kazan founded and headed the United Housing Foundation (UHF), a federation of housing cooperatives, civic groups, labor unions, and other nonprofit organizations, which became a leader in affordable housing. The UHF became responsible for vast tracts of New York rental apartments, including Co-op City in the Bronx, the largest cooperative housing project of its kind. By the time of Marina City's construction, the UHF had built 14,402 dwelling units, with another 11,625 under construction. This provided a possible model for McFetridge. Goldberg, though, was already familiar with this concept: "I have seen a great deal of Union housing in Europe as an architectural student. I have seen much housing done by the cooperative garment workers unions in New York."[20] However, no union projects of similar magnitude existed in Chicago.

Other labor leaders had also taken up this cause; by the early 1960s unions invested, as mortgage lenders, an estimated half-billion dollars in apartment buildings.[21] Perhaps the most notorious use of union funds in real estate projects was that of the International Brotherhood of Teamsters, who under the leadership of Jimmy Hoffa in the 1950s and '60s poured their pension funds into the Mafia-led development of Las Vegas. The motivation for unions to enter the housing market varied—for Kazan the goal was to produce the best accommodation for families and individuals who could not afford to pay mortgage deposits or the cost of market rents. McFetridge shared this ambition but also wanted to create jobs for the Janitors' Union—Marina City would provide work for at least one hundred janitors.[22] A loyal Daley supporter, he also wanted to assist in Chicago's downtown revitalization. At the time of Marina City's conception in 1959, urban dwellers were moving into suburban developments, aided by new highway infrastructures. For Goldberg and McFetridge this was problematic. "City center is basic to society," argued Goldberg.[23] Downtown living cut commute time, adding to leisure time—one of the main rationales for Marina City's mixed-use program and location was its proximity to cultural venues and institutions. As Marina City's marketing brochure suggested, "Walking and Thinking"—two key urban activities—were to be integral amenities of what the new complex had to offer.[24]

In 1959 Goldberg and Swibel found a dramatic and historic 3.1-acre site on the north bank of the Chicago River, between Dearborn and State streets. Occupying Chicago's Block No. 1, the site was one of the largest real estate holdings in downtown Chicago and had been owned by the Chicago and North Western Railway for nearly a century. Titled Block No. 1 in the original town of Chicago in 1833, it had been conveyed on July 5 of the same year by John L. Reynolds, governor of Illinois, to the heirs of Alexander Wolcott—the Indian agent at Fort Dearborn and husband of Ellen Marion Kinzie, daughter of Chicago's first permanent settler, John Kinzie. A former freight yard and public parking lot, by the 1950s it contained Chicago and North Western Railway's tracks to Navy Pier and the North Pier of the Terminal District. The Janitors' Union obtained an option on the land in 1959 and purchased it in 1960.

Design began in 1959. According to both Geoffrey Goldberg and Bertold "Bert" Weinberg the initial design was done in conjunction with Ferdinand "Fred" Severud at the office of Severud-Elstad-Krueger Associates in New York, and already at this stage it involved circular towers.[25] However, no written or drawn records exist of this phase. The design then transformed a number of times between 1959 and 1965. [Fig. 24]

The first schematic proposal dated June 1959 and titled Labor Center was a mixed-use complex with three round towers—two forty-story residential towers and a ten-story office tower, the so-called Building No. 3. A second proposal from mid-October, Scheme A, added a square auditorium next to the circular office building. The auditorium was fully embedded within an eight-story base that included boat storage, commercial space, a bowling alley, offices, and parking. A third proposal from late October, Scheme B, now featured a rectangular office building with a circular ramp transporting cars to parking on

Chronology

1959

June
- McFetridge discusses the project idea with Goldberg
- ∗ 1st scheme—three round towers (Labor Center)

August
- City of Chicago Department of Planning and Development confirms Marina City's conformity with Chicago Development Plan
- Chicago and Washington, D.C., FHA officials consider the proposal

September
- Option on land expires; Janitors' Union's executive board approves feasibility study
- Wall Street Journal article on Marina City
- Report to the Locals article informs Janitors' Union members of the project

October
- Marina City Building Corporation (MCBC) and North Marina City Building Corporation (NMCBC) established
- ∗ 2nd scheme—Scheme A—three round towers, theater embedded within section
- ∗ 3rd scheme—Scheme B—two round towers, theater not embedded in section

December
- Funds received from the Janitors' Union for stock certificates in MCBC
- Janitors' Union down payment for land
- ∗ Scheme B developed in more detail

1960

February
- Theater catenary form roof design in concrete
- ∗ 4th scheme—square towers for FHA submittal
- Final versions of apartment plans
- Exhibition of Marina City at the Astor Hotel in New York City
- Project cost estimated at $36 million

June
- FHA mortgage insurance approval

July
- Foundation borings begin

September
- Continental Illinois National Bank and Trust Company confirmed as lender for construction loan

October
- $2 million loan agreement with General Electric

1960 (continued)

November
- Groundbreaking

December–January
- ∗ Contract A, B drawings completed based on 3rd scheme

1961

March
- ∗ 3rd scheme, Planned Urban Development approval
- Chicago newspaper articles claim building boom due to Marina City
- Marina City is published in a Moscow magazine

June
- Sullivan begins raising issues about governance and funding
- McFetridge threatens sale of Local 1's assets

July
- $5 million Continental Illinois National Bank and Trust Company loan for commercial construction agreed

September
- Three carpenters die in a scaffolding accident

October
- First dated detailed theater proposal

1962

January
- Show apartments and office showroom open

March
- Marina City construction photos published in Swiss magazine Bâtir

June
- Six workers injured in a hoist accident

July
- Second potential Chicago Marina City project, with car ramps publicized

August
- Lease for top floor of offices signed with radio station WCFL

September
- Tenancy of National Design Center announced

October
- First tenants move into east tower

December
- Marina City published in German magazine Die Neue Heimat

1963

January
- First tenants move into the west tower
- Model apartments open in Marina City
- Marina City Bank announced as tenant

February
- First passenger car housed in radial garage

1964

February–July
- Work on office building continues

March
- Ice rink opens

July
- Announcement of buyout of Janitors' Union, Local 32B and Pension Trust investment by Swibel

September
- Repair work to apartments

December
- Theater plan sketch includes television stages
- National Design Center opening

1965

January–April
- Design of theater continues

1966

January
- WFLD starts broadcasting from the theater building, where they have two large studios—with additional space in the office building

June
- Medicare rents space in office building

1967

February
- Theater detail design work continues

June
- Theater construction completed

its roof deck and a theater projecting above a two-story base. BGA drew up a variant of Scheme A in November 1959 but without the round office building. By December, the project was close to its final concept comprising two round residential towers, a rectangular office building, and a spatula-shaped theater plan; the first apartment plans had been completed (see Fig. 39).

In February 1960, BGA prepared the same proposal but with two square towers—this strategically conservative version was taken to the FHA in Washington, D.C., and was abandoned after FHA approval was gained. Scheme A received Planned Urban Development approval on March 14, 1961, but parts of the office building continued to change. Until October 1962 the office building had glazing extending to all four facades. The residential tower circular core—which had to accommodate typical "square" programs, such as chutes, elevators, and stairways—was a particular design challenge. Many schemes were developed, ultimately resulting in custom elevators accommodating the core's curvature.

Difficulties in finding a tenant delayed the architectural resolution of the theater building, allowing BGA to explore different structural solutions. In December 1959, in the tradition of Félix Candela and Pier Luigi Nervi, a rising saddle-shaped concrete roof was to "float" above a sheer glass entry wall to the theater lobby. This concept remained through all revisions, but the saddle shape changed in section over time. The first proposal followed the form of a catenary curve in long section, allowing for the tallest volume above the stage, but the short sections were arched and a sling-shaped concrete ring beam carried the load of the concrete roof (for the evolution of the theater building section, see Figs. 37 and 38). This beam was supported by concrete walls. The load of the cantilevered facade was carried by the concrete slab above the entrance lobby then down onto the square grid of columns on the base platform. It was an ambitious structural solution, particularly, as in early plans, the balcony floor plan was U-shaped and therefore could not act as a tie restraining the midplan horizontal forces of the roof. An October 1961 version of the theater also included a fully glazed facade facing Dearborn Street.

The theater roof design was revised at least four times. Detailed proposals for the building occupied the office in 1963, not only to resolve structural issues but also to accommodate different theater seating plans, suggesting interest from a specific tenant. However, no records exist of a potential tenant at that time. The design continued to change until WFLD finally signed the lease in 1965 when television stages were incorporated. The final design changed from concrete to steel, although it is not clear whether this was a cost or a structural issue. The exuberant saddle-shape remained, though with a shallower curve in long section and more vertical structure beneath.

Given the scale and complexity of the project, the design and construction periods were impressively short. The timeline, opposite, defines key moments in the history of the project. [Fig. 24]

Five distinct structures make up the Marina City complex: two residential towers, a saddle-shaped auditorium building, and a ten-story office building. All of these sit on top of the fifth and final structure—a raised commercial platform covering the entire site but also straddling the railway below and divided into north and south components. [Fig. 25] The building's total area is 1.8 million square feet. Goldberg designed the complex for high-density living—a true "city within a city"—encompassing a breadth of programs: theater, a gym, a swimming pool, an ice rink, a bowling alley, a boat marina, shopping, restaurants, offices,

←

24. Timeline representing the duration of key time periods from 1959 to 1967 in Marina City's design and construction.

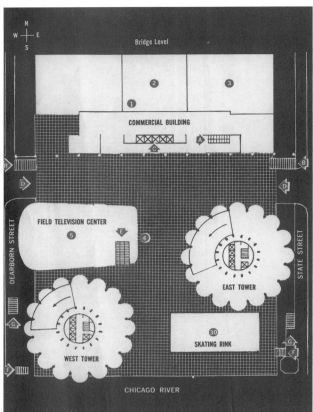

Bridge Level

COMMERCIAL BUILDING

N W E S

DEARBORN STREET

FIELD TELEVISION CENTER

EAST TOWER

WEST TOWER

SKATING RINK

STATE STREET

CHICAGO RIVER

Marina City Map Locations

Commercial Building Bridge Level
1. Marina City Copying Service
2. Marina City Drugs & Liquors
3. Marina City Bank

Street Level
6. Health Club and Swimming Pool
7. Barber Shop
8. Ladies' Room
9. Men's Room
10. Marina City Valet Service
11. Beauty Salon
12. Tunnel Connecting Residential and Commercial Buildings

Field Television Center Bridge Level
4. Parking Cashier— Main Entrance
5. WFLD—Channel 32

Street Level
13. McFetridge Hall auditorium—exhibition hall

Residential Towers Lobby
14. Teleview Teller
15. Faber's Tobacco and Gift Shop
16. Small World Travel Service
17. Marina City Management Office
18. Package Room
19. Information Desk
20. Marina City Flowers by Villari
21. Stromberg DatagraphiX Display
22. Checkroom
23. Public Telephones

LEGEND:
To go from the Commercial Building to the Residential Towers Lobby, take the stairs or elevators down to the street level and cross the tunnel to the lobby.

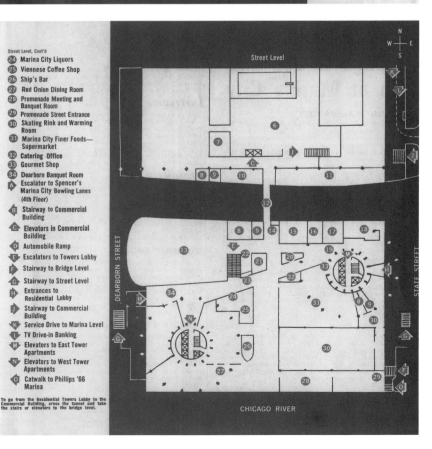

Street Level, Cont'd
24. Marina City Liquors
25. Viennese Coffee Shop
26. Ship's Bar
27. Red Onion Dining Room
28. Promenade Meeting and Banquet Room
29. Promenade Street Entrance
30. Skating Rink and Warming Room
31. Marina City Finer Foods— Supermarket
32. Catering Office
33. Gourmet Shop
34. Dearborn Banquet Room
A. Escalator to Spencer's Marina City Bowling Lanes (4th Floor)
B. Stairway to Commercial Building
C. Elevators in Commercial Building
D. Automobile Ramp
E. Escalators to Towers Lobby
F. Stairway to Bridge Level
G. Stairway to Street Level
H. Entrances to Residential Lobby
J. Stairway to Commercial Building
K. Service Drive to Marina Level
L. TV Drive-in Banking
M. Elevators to East Tower Apartments
N. Elevators to West Tower Apartments
O. Catwalk to Phillips '66 Marina

To go from the Residential Towers Lobby to the Commercial Building, cross the tunnel and take the stairs or elevators to the bridge level.

Street Level

N W E S

DEARBORN STREET

STATE STREET

CHICAGO RIVER

50

a bank, a television station, parking, and housing.[26] It also included services such as a beauty shop, a barber shop, a tailor shop, a newsstand, a florist, and bookshop.[27] There was even a plan to include the Janitors' Union's health clinic.[28] Landscape design by Alfred Caldwell—a regular collaborator with BGA and a significant Chicago landscape architect—and artwork by prominent international artists, such as Victor Vasarely, in the Marina City theater lobby, added to the complex's progressive design image.

The Towers

When completed, Marina City's apartment towers were the tallest concrete and residential structures in the world, with clearly expressed curvilinear concrete balconies. Goldberg described each as a "tremendous tree trunk."[29] Their asymmetrical siting on the podium provides a counterpoint to their sinuous structural symmetry. The curves of the balcony floors, flowing smoothly into vertical columns, represent a seamless transition between and integration of architectural and engineering decisions. [Fig. 26] Goldberg thought that rectilinear housing projects were depressing. He said, "(I) wanted to get people out of boxes, which are really psychological slums," adding, "Those long hallways with scores of doors opening anonymously are inhuman. Each person should retain his own relation to the core. It should be the relation of the branch to the tree, rather than that of the cell to the honeycomb."[30]

Residents entered the apartment complex either through the theater's glass lobby and down the escalators into the commercial platform's broad corridor connecting the tower lobbies, or through street level doors on Dearborn and State streets directly into the corridor. The central core of each sixty-story tower connects to a total of 896 apartments on the top forty floors. The first eighteen floors contain parking ramps with separate circulation. The first residential tenants moved into the east tower of Marina City on October 14, 1962, and into the west tower on January 12, 1963.[31] The apartments varied in size, with 256 efficiency units, 576 one-bedroom and, on the top ten floors, 64 two-bedroom units. [Fig. 27] The density was high with three hundred families per acre. All apartments were originally rentals but were converted to condominiums in 1977.

The circular arrangement of the central core avoids the institutional look of conventional double-loaded corridors found in many hotels and large-scale housing projects. The circular corridor was low-lit to save energy, with finishes and individual door colors to enhance orientation. The cores contain five elevators, fire stairs, plumbing and electrical lines, electrical transformers, a trash chute, and utility rooms. A smoke shaft—to which louvers from the core staircases would open in case of fire—is also integrated.

From the circular central core, ringed by the access corridor, Marina City apartment plans radiate in the form of sixteen "petals." An efficiency apartment occupies one petal, a one-bedroom unit occupies a petal and a half, while a two-bedroom unit occupies two and a half petals. Each petal's radial geometry is subtle, with a gentle outward flare. The bathroom and kitchen are close to the core and next to the entry, while living and sleeping quarters extend to the balcony. This reduces utility distribution lines and locates darker areas inward, while opening living and sleeping quarters to the sun.

Marina City's pièce de résistance is the balcony—a spacious exterior space with unobstructed views of Chicago. The floor-to-ceiling glass facade and balcony compensated for the FHA-mandated low square footage.

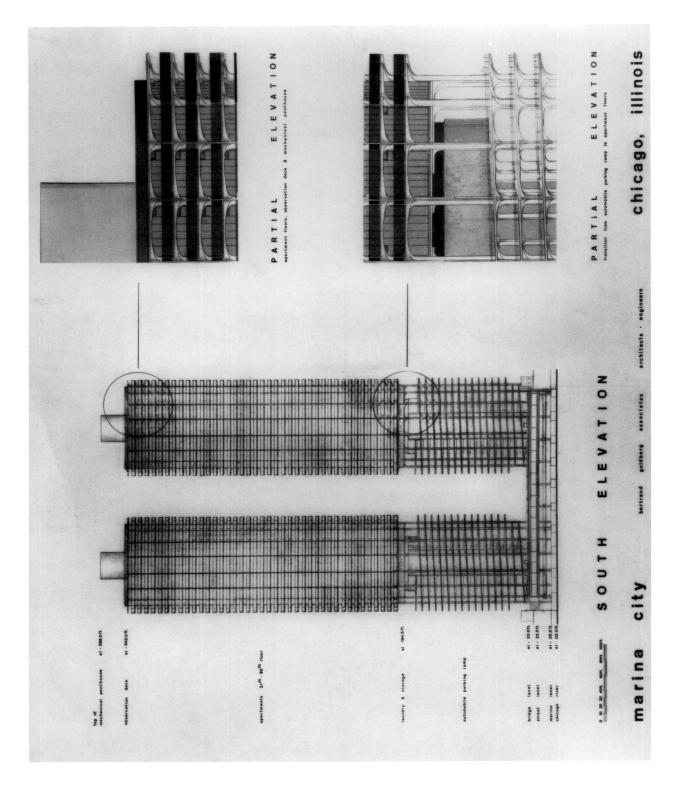

PARTIAL ELEVATION
apartment floors, observation deck & mechanical penthouse

PARTIAL ELEVATION
transition from automobile parking ramp to apartment floors

chicago, illinois

SOUTH ELEVATION   bertrand goldberg associates   architects · engineers

top of
mechanical penthouse   el · 588.0 ft.

observation deck   el · 543.0 ft.

apartments 21st - 60th floor

laundry & storage   el · 194.5 ft.

automobile parking ramp

bridge level   el · 33.0 ft.
street level   el · 22.0 ft.
marina level   el · 05.0 ft.
chicago river   el · 02.0 ft.

0 10 20 30 40ft. 60ft. 80ft. 100ft.

marina city

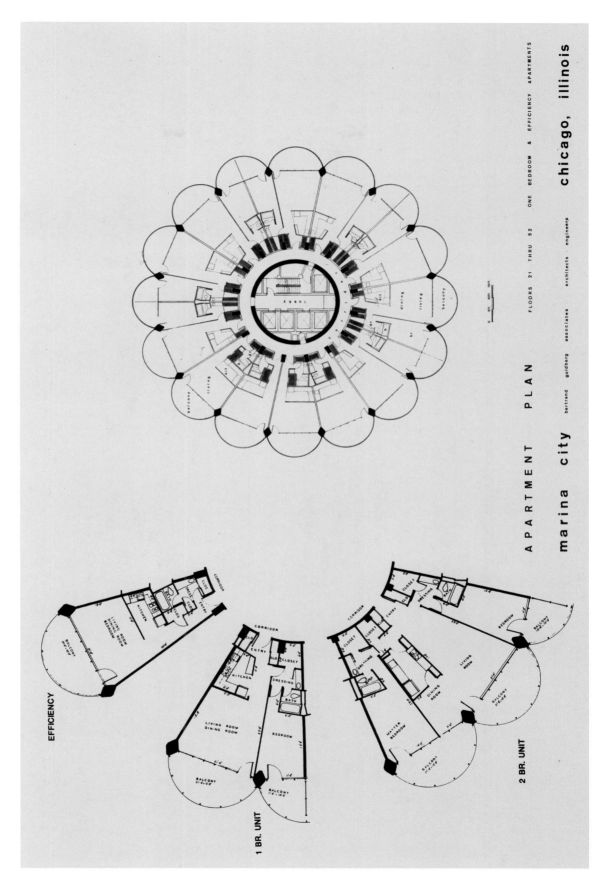

APARTMENT PLAN

marina city

chicago, illinois

FLOORS 21 THRU 52   ONE BEDROOM & EFFICIENCY APARTMENTS

bertrand goldberg associates   architects   engineers

EFFICIENCY

1 BR. UNIT

2 BR. UNIT

BGA carefully studied the balconies in a full-scale mock-up to avoid them being used as storage areas, a common occurrence in Chicago apartment buildings. The living room shares a large glazed wall with the balcony, making the balcony its visual and programmatic extension. [Fig. 28] The balcony space elegantly frames views of the city. The center of its semicircular plan is more than six feet away from the apartment glass walls; this, together with the sheltering effect of its curvilinear cantilevered horizontal floor and ceiling slabs, also provides visual security. A delicate four-foot-tall railing and a dropped perimeter concrete edge beam above define the edge. The balcony also makes air-conditioning equipment maintenance and window washing easy.

The interior design in Marina City's showroom and model apartments discussed in "The Image" chapter highlighted an interesting duality of American residential architecture at the time by integrating modernist architecture with traditional furniture and conservative decorative patterns. In the kitchens, dressing rooms, and bathrooms, the latest furniture and the newest technological gadgets dominated; in the living rooms and bedrooms more classical interior features, such as traditional rugs and covers, subtly balanced the stark modernity of the building. Marina City model apartments captured in Hedrich-Blessing photographs emphasize this duality.

The bedroom plan allowed compact modern furniture to be placed in a variety of layouts, framed by the structurally expressive beams. [Fig. 29] The integration of media and technology was most visible in the bedroom. Tenants could stay in touch with news and control their environment with electrical gadgets including "a portable television, temperature control box within easy reach and a handy telephone. All the Marina City apartment rooms have combined electrical outlets and telephone jacks within reach of any possible furniture arrangement."[32]

A photograph of a study area also showed television sets and telephones, highlighting the importance of media in everyday life: "The breakfast bar in the kitchen of the one-bedroom apartment is a perfect spot for that quick cup of coffee breakfast while watching the morning news, or just for an 'anytime' snack."[33] [Fig. 30]

The kitchens were all-electric, fitted with General Electric appliances, including garbage disposal units and Textolite-coated countertops. [Fig. 31] The built-in steel kitchen cabinets were finished in vibrant pastel colors, such as yellow and aquamarine. With Marina City's immense scale, elements that would normally have been custom-detailed could be mass-produced. The kitchens had outlets and space for contemporary electrical equipment such as blenders and toasters. An image of the Marina City kitchen even showed wallpaper with a pattern that appeared to be based on the Marina City floor plan. Upon closer examination the wallpaper was actually based on alternating patterns of whole and sliced oranges.

The bathrooms, with a toilet and bathtub, were efficiently planned and fitted with up-to-date appliances and had floor-to-ceiling small glass mosaic tiles in vibrant colors (yellows, reds, and greens). [Fig. 32] Their delicate pattern and reflectivity created an abstract checkerboard effect, dissolving some of the materiality of the tight space. In keeping with the overall aesthetic, ventilation ducts and recessed lights were circular. The circular light above the toilet, inserted in a small area of dropped ceiling, hid the toilet waste pipe on the floor above—avoiding an increase in ceiling height. The adjacent dressing room vanity incorporated phone and electrical outlets in its custom-built elements—

28. Apartment interior with couple on balcony, Marina City (1959–1967), Bertrand Goldberg Associates, Chicago, IL. Hedrich-Blessing [photographer]. HB-23215-I3, Chicago History Museum.

29. Bedroom, Marina City (1959–1967), Bertrand Goldberg Associates, Chicago, IL. Hedrich-Blessing [photographer]. HB-23215-F3, Chicago History Museum.

30. Study area in a two-bedroom model apartment at Marina City, Marina City (1959–1967), Bertrand Goldberg Associates, Chicago, IL. Hedrich-Blessing [photographer]. HB-23215-L3, Bertrand Goldberg Archive, Ryerson and Burnham Archives, The Art Institute of Chicago. Courtesy of The Art Institute of Chicago. © The Chicago History Museum

31. Apartment kitchen, Marina City (1959–1967), Bertrand Goldberg Associates, Chicago, IL. Hedrich-Blessing [photographer]. HB-23215-E2, Bertrand Goldberg Archive, Ryerson and Burnham Archives, The Art Institute of Chicago. Courtesy of The Art Institute of Chicago. © The Chicago History Museum

32. Bathroom, Marina City (1959–1967), Bertrand Goldberg Associates, Chicago, IL. Hedrich-Blessing [photographer]. HB-23215-P2, Chicago History Museum.

a dressing table, clothes drawers, and a closet—in steel, stainless steel, chrome-plated steel, mirror glass, and molded plastic.

The residential towers also had laundry rooms and storage on the twentieth floor, located between the parking spiral and the apartments. The laundry room featured floor-to-ceiling glass and unobstructed city views. The helical parking structure provided 896 parking spaces, one for each apartment. The lowest two floors are steeper to hold cars before they are parked. From the fifth floor upwards the ramps slope at only 5 percent, a safer angle. The parking spaces were planned for valet parking, and a small hoist lift moves the car valets up and down the building quickly without using the central core elevators, which are not connected to the parking ramps.[34] Special drains prevent spilled gasoline from spreading across the ramp. Cars are parked one-deep, never more than fifty feet from the valet lifts. This single-slot parking system and the proximity to valet lifts reduces waiting time and eliminates damage to cars, an occurence common to traditional multilayer car parks.

Finally, residents have access to a roof deck, whose main area is clear of mechanical equipment. The deck is used for special events and provides dramatic city views from its entire perimeter.

Office Building

The ten-story office building visually shields Marina City from the jumble of buildings to the north and anchors the edge of the complex. Below it sits a long, solid horizontal two-story block containing a bowling alley, with a a fully glazed floor on the entry level below and a roof deck promenade above on the fourth level. The office building, resting on in situ concrete groin vaults, thus rises from the fifth to the fifteenth floor. The vaults arch outward to support the office building in a visual analogy to the curvatures of other structures within the complex (see Fig. 53).

The building provided more than 170,000 square feet of flexible rental office space. It contained a central core with mechanical services—five elevators, two stairways, and bathrooms—allowing for maximum flexibility in floor layouts. [Figs. 33 and 34] A typical floor plan provided offices for prospective tenants with options for open plan or cellular office space configured as a double-loaded corridor. The tenants also had partial control over building systems—all-electric lighting, heating, and cooling systems could be modified by each tenant—similar to the individual controls in the residential tower. The light fixtures were carefully designed to provide even illumination for all working surfaces. The building did not, however, rely solely on electric lighting. The narrow footprint meant that no work area was farther than thirty feet from the window, allowing natural light to directly reach a minimum of half the floor area.

Unlike a suburban office park, whose value depended on its proximity to highways, Marina City offered the option of living and working in the same block, eliminating commuting stress. It was part of a larger urban network of housing, commercial, and cultural facilities that intertwined conceptually and financially; office tenants were invited to take advantage of the nearby theater for meetings and presentations. Marina City also offered contemporary necessities such as parking, conveniently located in the residential towers. A structure made to accomodate car culture, it also drew upon historical notions of public space and urban density.

The rectilinear geometry of the office building with its narrow cast-in-place concrete mullions, created a repetitive vertical facade pattern as tight and as

overleaf, p. 58 →
33. Office building, typical floor plan, Marina City (1959–1967), Bertrand Goldberg Associates, Chicago, IL, 1962. Bertrand Goldberg Archive, Architecture and Design Department, Art Institute of Chicago.

overleaf, p. 59 → →
34. Office building, south facade, Marina City (1959–1967), Bertrand Goldberg Associates, Chicago, IL, 1963. Bertrand Goldberg Archive, Architecture and Design Department, Art Institute of Chicago.

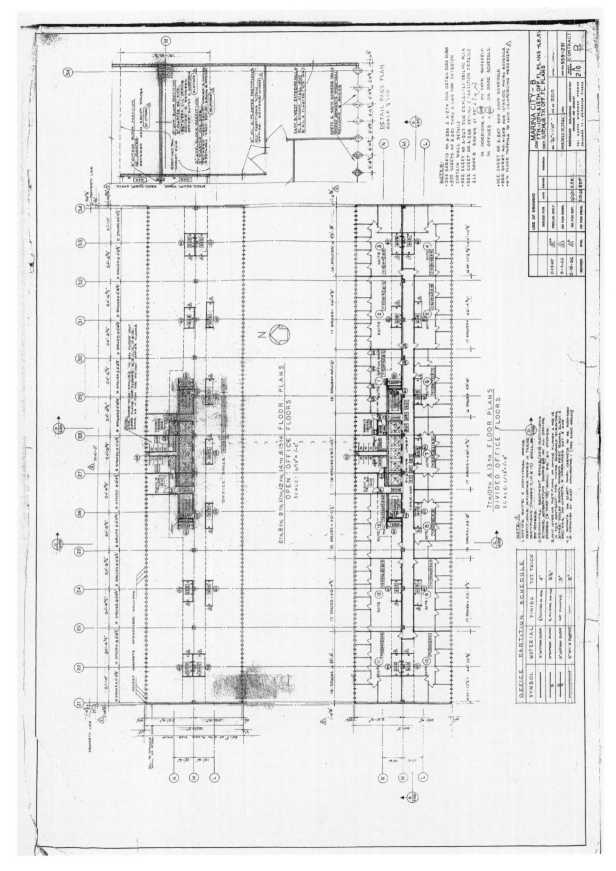

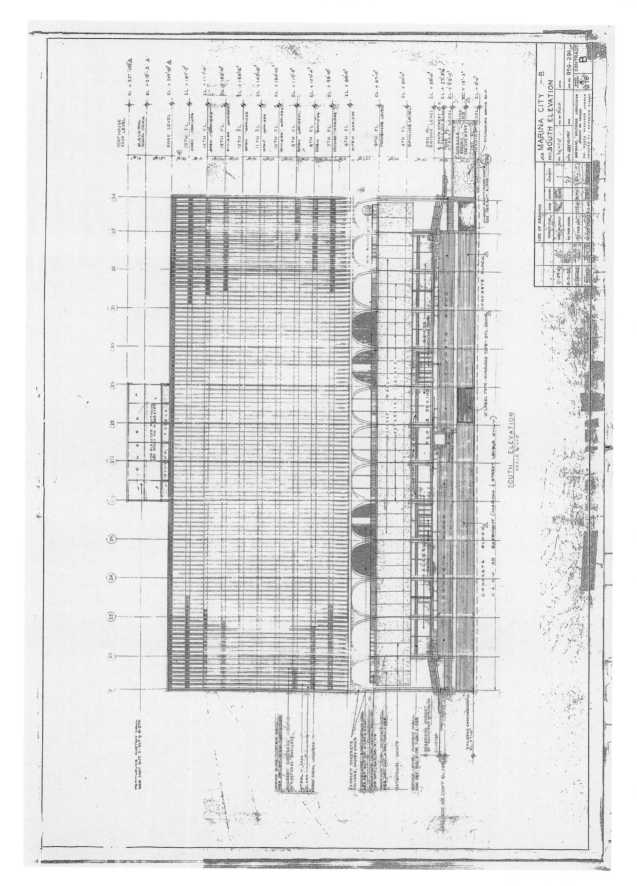

SOUTH ELEVATION
SCALE ¼" = 1'-0"

**35. Office building, Marina City
(1959–1967), Bertrand Goldberg
Associates, Chicago, IL, mid-1960s.**
Orlando Cabanban [photographer]. Bertrand Goldberg
Archive, Ryerson and Burnham Archives, The Art Institute
of Chicago. Digital File #200203.081229-325
© The Art Institute of Chicago.

**36. Office building, interior, Marina
City (1959–1967), Bertrand Goldberg
Associates, Chicago, IL.** Orlando Cabanban
[photographer]. Bertrand Goldberg Archive, Ryerson
and Burnham Archives, The Art Institute of Chicago.
Digital File #200203.081229-335 © The Art Institute
of Chicago.

minimal as the curvilinear balconies of the residential towers were sinuous and exuberant. [Fig. 35] If the exterior form of the towers alluded to organic figures made of soft, circular protrusions, the office building alluded to the concrete equivalent of a pin-striped suit—a "masculine" counterpart to the towers' organic form. Yet the office building's form and spaces were more nuanced: the pilotis-like groin vaults created an extraordinary gothic space between the office tower base and the deck promenade (see Fig. 53). Equally intriguing, the concrete mullions had an undulating kidney-shaped profile; yet as they covered the entire facade, their softness dissolved into a disciplined repetitive pattern (see Fig. 57). Clearly showing evidence of both Goldberg's "humanism" and the individual hand at work, these spaces suggested both formally and in terms of construction technique a meeting of the rationality of industrial construction processes with the disciplined craftsmanship of a Gothic cathedral. At the same time, their open, airy, and well-lit interiors provided an efficient and flexible space that easily could be adjusted to individual tenants' needs, including those of the BGA office. [Fig. 36]

An early tenant was the National Design Center. Founded by a New York–based furniture retailer Norman Ginsberg, it was the first commercial tenant to open its premises in the office building at the end of 1964.[35] Its exhibitions of building products, appliances, furnishings, and fabrics embodied the same progressive ideas about design as the complex itself. Occupying four floors, the National Design Center had an auditorium, a bookstore, and temporary exhibition areas open to the public and to design professionals. Its library and information bureau supplied publications and advice about design products and services to designers and to consumers. A November 1964 issue of *Inland Architect* featured the National Design Center in a special multipage section: "Within its four floors in Marina City, the National Design Center projects a dual aesthetic role, both visional and visual, creative and functional, as the inspiring symbol of excellence in design and as the motivating nucleus for good design in industry. Chicago is the natural hub of innovation."[36]

The choice of the Marina City office building for the National Design Center was not coincidental. The complex was seen as a symbol of total (modern) design—integrating engineering, architecture, interior design, and urban design. George Danforth, IIT College of Architecture dean after Mies, and a partner in Brenner-Danforth-Rockwell, the designers of the National Design Center's interior, said in his oral history that their design work had started while the office building was still under construction. Brenner-Danforth-Rockwell received the American Institute of Architects (AIA) Chicago Citation of Merit for New Buildings in 1966.[37] Yet the National Design Center closed a few years after its opening, in part due to competition from the nearby Merchandise Mart.

Theater

The theater building, located north of the west residential tower, forms the third component of Marina City. Its structure, like that of the towers, is curvilinear and symmetrical. The saddle-shaped and lead-clad form would have seemed heavy were it not for "hovering" above the entrance lobby made of glass on three of its four sides. This glass base lifted the theater building and visually disconnected it from the ground, like a saddle, reinforcing its conceptual and formal autonomy. Its descriptive geometry was systematically determined by Richard Ayliffe "Dick" Binfield, a BGA employee whose gift for precise, spidery lines

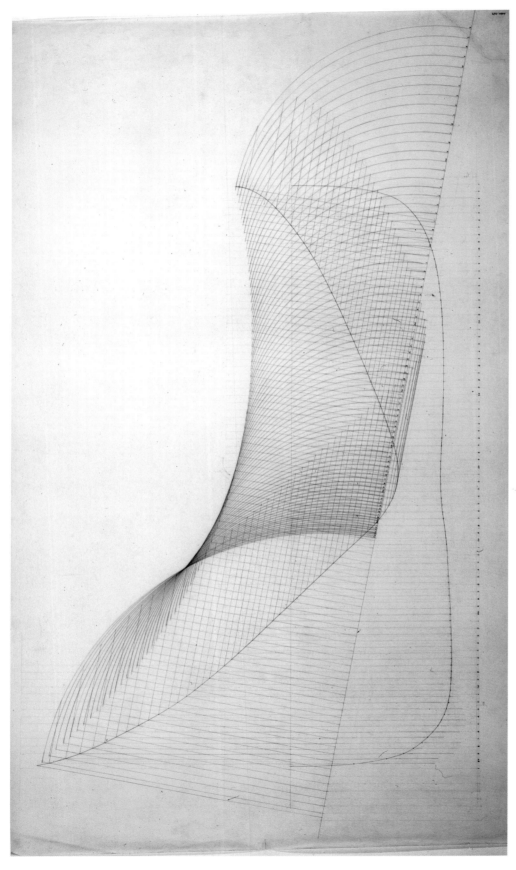

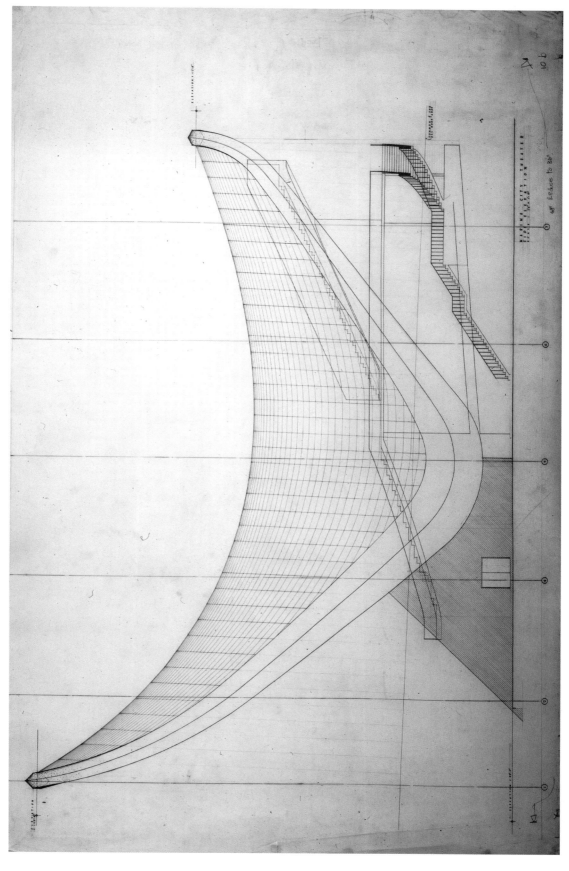

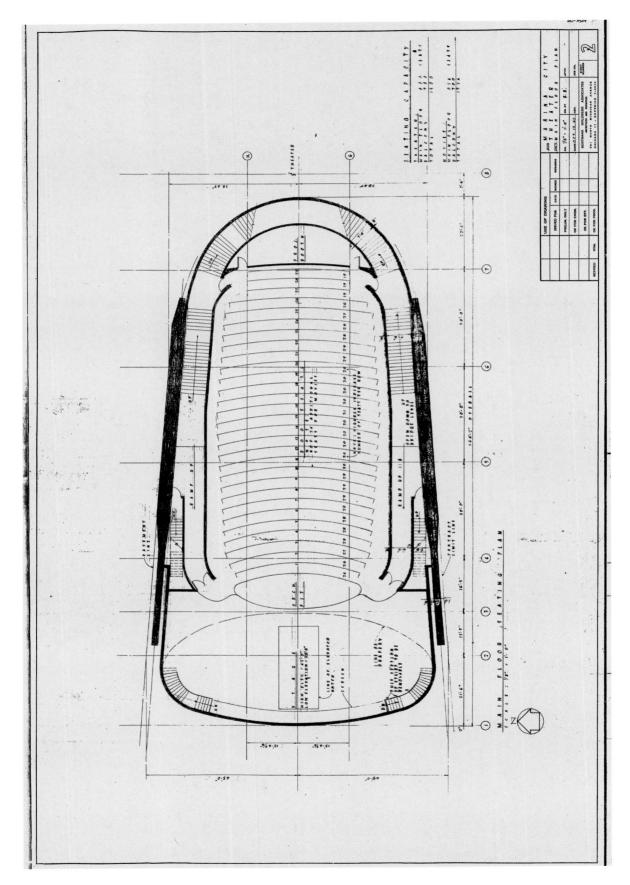

MAIN FLOOR SEATING PLAN
SCALE: 1/8" = 1'-0"

also showed determination to establish the right roof curvature and its impact on structural members. [**Figs. 37–39**]

Tucked inbetween the towers and the office building, the theater building was somewhat concealed within the core of the complex. [**Fig. 40**] However, it played an important programmatic role—it was the main entry for Marina City's residential towers. Amidst glittering reflections bouncing off the seamless glass facade of its lobby, residents and visitors arriving by car approached the complex. [**Fig. 41**] After valet parking, they entered the lobby and continued down the escalators to the main apartment towers' lobbies located on the level below. The theater building, rather than the side entrances on State and Dearborn streets thus formed the main formal gateway to the residential and commercial spaces. This suggests that the arched facade above the glass lobby that the saddle-shaped roof presented to the Marina City plaza was not only a functional expression of its program but also a formal expression of its doorlike quality.

The building was planned to hold a 1,200-seat theater (expandable to 2,400 seats by opening to lower level exhibition and meeting spaces) and a 700-seat auditorium. Originally to be named McFetridge Hall, the auditorium sat piggyback on smaller theaters beneath. It was changed into a broadcasting facility for WFLD in the mid-1960s when the large space became a television studio and the two smaller theaters below operated as movie theaters. Particular attention was paid to acoustics; BGA planned to cover the theater ceiling with plastic domes that could be inflated and deflated from the projection booth, thus controlling sound quality. The main theater was the first ever designed specifically for the showing of wide-screen pictures. The wide screen was suspended against a 92-foot-high wall without a proscenium arch, and behind the screen a 90-foot-tall black curtain brightened the corners of the picture screen for better image quality. The theater building was envisioned as Marina City's entertainment zone, a hub for movies, concerts, community meetings, and other public events. It was also envisioned as an extension of the Marina City office building, since the auditorium and lobby spaces provided venues for sales presentations and business gatherings.

Commercial Platform

The fourth element of the project is the commercial platform covering the entire three-acre lot. Sometimes also referred to as "the base building" by Goldberg, it is a one-story rectangular block with an open plaza as its roof and a boat marina beneath. Functionally and symbolically it locates leisure, entertainment, and business as the programmatic base of the complex. Within its rectangular form there was a final, if minor, spatial intervention—the negative space of the skating rink, excavated down a level to be viewed from both restaurant and plaza levels. [Fig. 42] Although no longer part of the Marina City complex, the skating rink was one of its main marketing features. To be used year-round, it was protected with a retractable canvas roof that covered the skating surface during inclement winter weather. Another outdoor feature of the plaza was Alfred Caldwell's small garden, its soft green texture complementing the adjacent hard concrete surfaces. [Fig. 43]

The commercial platform is a pedestal, with the towers, office, and theater "floating" to some degree as sculptural objects above its horizontal plane. The different structural geometries necessarily continue through the platform's two stories to permit structural loads to transfer to foundations. Beneath the plaza lurk the structural and mechanical feeder systems of the complex, as well as the most complex part of the programming. It comprised restaurants, a store, a health club, an ice rink, and so on—all inserted in, and intertwined with, the structural and service geometries of the elements above. Heating, ventilation, air conditioning, plumbing, electrical, telephone, and other systems extend like gigantic roots through the platform and are diverted to accommodate other, lower-level rootlike systems—the railway, the delivery road, and the marina docks. The marina below the commercial level, with easy access to the Chicago River and Lake Michigan, is available for the use of Marina City residents and other users. A crane removes boats from the water and stores them in adjacent storage racks located deep in the complex. Like the other buildings positioned above it, the commercial platform rests on pilotis between which boats dock negating the solidity of its formal function and form. In a second formal contradiction, the

continuous glass plane along the podium's river facade further undermines the idea of a stable, solid base. The decision to site all elements of the complex on top of the commercial platform caused some practical problems of use and servicing, giving the platform's construction plans their appearance of a warren crawling with environmental systems.

City within a City

Marina City's rich urban mix was unprecedented for Chicago, and its architectural design was unique. Design elements, such as the parking ramp, quickly became iconic. Thus, where Wright used spiral movement in the Guggenheim Museum (1959) to represent the process of viewing high art, Goldberg expressed the dynamic form of automobile transportation in Marina City's parking ramp, an important marketing aspect of the project.

Goldberg also drew inspiration from traditional civic models, such as public buildings of the late Middle Ages.[38] Nowhere else was this merger of mixed function, density, and human encounters more elaborately developed within the complex than in the Marina City commercial platform—a network of amenities connecting the separate elements of Marina City. The platform concept built upon important historical precedents such as Rockefeller Center (1939) and the Auditorium Building. It was to be an open semipublic space, substituting traditional street fronts for a classical forum concept.

The commercial platform contained a variety of programs and services, including the apartment tower lobbies, shops, banks, security controls, a cashier's counter for parking business, a package room, a mail room, a newspaper stand, a commissary, a drugstore, a restaurant and so on. [Figs. 44 and 45] All of these complemented programs and services were located in other parts of the complex. The commercial platform programs facing the river included the restaurant, meeting, and banquet rooms and capitalized on city views through their glass facade. The platform extends, via a bridge over the railway, under the office building where it included a health club with a swimming pool and steam room.

The solid two-story slab at the base of the office building included other programs and services, such as the enormous bowling alley with fifty-four bowling lanes. [Fig. 46] Its recreational promenade deck on the second floor is an outdoor amenity for its tenants.

For those longing for high altitudes there are also roof decks on top of the residential towers. These spaces were intentionally left unprogrammed and were appropriated for everyday activities such as lounging, grilling, conversing, and relaxing.

"The House the Janitors Built" emerged out of the aspirations of labor yet celebrated the city as a center for leisure and consumption.[39] Marina City's embodiment of the pursuit of pleasure was perhaps best exemplified in an image of the Malmö Girls, a Swedish rhythmic gymnastic group exercising and posing on the roof deck during their 1965 visit to the complex, documented in a contemporary *Marina City Newsletter*.[40] [Fig. 47] The coordinated performance of their athletic bodies represented not only the role of Marina City spaces for accommodating entertainment, but also it resonated with the sinuous skyward structure of its key architectural components—a vision of vertical mobility and weightlessness appropriate for the space exploration age.

the structure

BERTRAND GOLDBERG'S MARINA CITY ... IS A STUNNING EXHI-
BITION OF THE UNPARALLELED AND INEXHAUSTIBLE POWER
IN THE CITY'S GREAT BUILDING TRADITION.

—CARL W. CONDIT, *THE CHICAGO SCHOOL OF ARCHITECTURE*

When completed in 1964, the two towers of Marina City were both the tallest
residential buildings and the highest reinforced concrete structures in the world.
Built in the spirit of Chicago's vast infrastructural works, its designers' architectural and engineering ambition immediately positioned it within Chicago's
architectural history. Their design and engineering served not only their ideal of
progressive living but also their ideal of affordability, which in turn drove both
construction sequencing and management decisions. A remarkable study in
formal elegance, structural efficiency, and organizational precision—a textbook
example of the integration of architectural, engineering, construction, and service systems—Marina City is the result of an efficient architectural, engineering,
and construction team.

Architects

Bertrand Goldberg Associates were the dynamo behind Marina City's design,
engineering, and construction sequencing. The office also provided quirky but
important solutions in which mass-production met individual craftsmanship. This
is all the more impressive given that the office had not previously built anything
similar in scope and size to Marina City.

Bertrand Goldberg's European and North American education had forged
his broad understanding of architectural practice. Through his initial fascination
with systems and his practice's gradual growth, Goldberg was able to quickly
create and manage an appropriate division of labor within the office—also a
result of the complex client and contractor relationships developed through its
wartime projects. The office took a great deal of care over every detail, both in
design and construction. Paint thickness meters, moisture meters, and surveying machines were taken to the site on a regular basis.

←

48. Tower core as seen from the Loop,
Marina City (1959–1967), Bertrand
Goldberg Associates, Chicago, IL,
September 1961. Richard Nickel [photographer].
Courtesy of the Richard Nickel Committee, Chicago,
Illinois. Bertrand Goldberg Archive, Ryerson and Burnham
Archives, The Art Institute of Chicago. © The Art
Institute of Chicago.

Other architects—Ben Honda and Richard Ayliffe "Dick" Binfield, and later Edward "Ed" Center and Albert "Al" Goers—formed the core of the office. Ed Center was the office's most senior and trusted associate. He dealt with all the contract packaging and the integration of design and construction. He did not run construction, design, or production, but he followed all the parts as they came together and was a highly effective contributor to the management of complex projects. Ben Honda joined BGA in late 1959, after working for Pace Associates, Mies van der Rohe's working-drawing office. He had studied at IIT on the GI Bill and was a skilled draftsman; he made fabricator study models for the contractor that explained how to make curved concrete surfaces.[1] Binfield was heavily involved in programming and drew the many Marina City theater drawings. In particular the complex curvature of both the first and final theater roof required many detailed iterations, all drawn by Binfield.

Also working for the office, but not in positions of responsibility, were a younger generation of largely Chicago-trained architects. In 1960 Louis Rocah joined the office, after studing under Mies at IIT and working under Walter Netsch on Skidmore, Owings and Merrill's (SOM) Air Force Academy Chapel (1956–1962) in Colorado Springs, Colorado. Rocah had "honesty and good eyes," and at the age of only twenty-five Goldberg trusted him to go out in the field.[2] Bernie Babka joined the office shortly after Ben Honda, closely followed by Ed Center. Though critical judgment was reserved for the first tier of staff, the office also had an important second staff contingent. This group included Joe Burnett, who assisted with drawings, and Maglet Myhrum and "Dutch" Bouchelle, both female architects, who were responsible for interiors.[3] With Elaine Hayano, as well as Shirley Miller, the office secretary, they were the female employees of the office.

A further group completed the office. By 1960 BGA employed ten to twelve architects, about eight structural engineers, and half a dozen engineers each in the mechanical and electrical departments; most had been hired to work on Marina City.[4] The teams were fully integrated. Their chiefs met every morning to share and solve problems and drove Marina City's successful synthesis of architecture, structure, services, and construction. An example of such coordination was the location of electrical conduit in the apartment floor slabs. Where the conduits crossed each other, the six-inch floor thickness was not enough to cover them, but the floors could not be thicker because the weight of the concrete would have been too much for the already built caissons. The architecture and electrical engineering chiefs agreed to locate the crossovers in those areas of the floor slab where partitions were to be located above and below.

Engineers

The initial engineering expertise for Marina City came from both Chicago and New York. From the beginning Goldberg had been working on the structural aspects of the proposal with the Norwegian-born engineer Fred Severud who was joined by Hannskarl Bandel, both of New York–based Severud-Elstad-Krueger Associates. The firm was known for its innovative solutions and ability to troubleshoot complex engineering problems. Goldberg's initial structural concept was based purely on a structural concrete core with apartment petals hung from it. Severud steered Goldberg away from this risky concept, suggesting a combination of a concrete core and columns on the periphery.[5] Goldberg eventually adopted this hybrid solution; it became evident already in Marina City's first scheme in 1959, which consisted of three circular towers.

Chicago engineers Bert Weinberg and Eugene "Gene" Yamamoto were also involved in the early designs; Frank Kornacker joined shortly after Weinberg. Ralph Bernardini had already been working in the office and had a professional engineering license, but Weinberg was the first full-time structural engineer. Trained at Rensselaer Polytechnic Institute on the GI Bill, he had worked for Frank Kornacker on the structural engineering for 860–880 Lakeshore Drive Apartments (1949) and joined BGA in 1958 to work on the Astor Tower; he left in 1963 after the structural work on the Marina City office building was completed. He had tremendous engineering skills with which he solved the problem of poor bearing at the base of the two towers. The east tower problem was solved by installing a three-foot-deep concrete mat and the west tower problem with a six-foot-deep one—simpler and cheaper solutions than the normal practice of casting caisson caps and connecting beams. The pouring of the six-foot concrete mat involved one of the first uses of ice in a concrete mix and, to stop the concrete from overheating, it was poured in a single nighttime session.

Weinberg hired Yamamoto, who remained in the office for many years. Kornacker joined the office in 1960; by that time the Marina City design was in full flow and the office had ten or more structural engineers.[6] External consultants included A. A. Fejfer, an IIT-trained engineer, who did the early wind load analysis; Sidney Berman, a research professor at the University of Illinois, investigated soil conditions; and Ralph Peck, also a research professor at the University of Illinois, and Moran, Proctor, Mueser & Rutledge, a New York consulting engineering firm, did foundation investigations. Wayne Teng, of the newly founded Teng and Associates, also provided structural engineering services to the project.[7] Robert O. Ritchie provided mechanical engineering consultancy services and New York–based construction management and cost consultants McKee-Berger-Mansueto worked on quantity surveying and cost estimates.

Contractors

The complexity of Marina City's construction required innovation and improvisation well beyond the office. Goldberg assembled, both within the office and on-site, an interesting collection of individuals with special skills. For example, Milo Ozuk—whose father had worked with Goldberg on a fiberglass car—solved various mechanical problems with his abilities as a fabricator and welder. Fred Zimmerman, a former Otis elevator engineer, looked at the elevator proposals—in early drawings these were standard but were eventually custom-made with a cut corner to fit the circular core. However, Goldberg's experience and interest in construction management remained central to the structural and constructional innovations in the project.

The most important organization working on-site was that of the main contractor. Marina City's fast and efficient construction was realized through innovative bidding. Anticipating today's process of fast-tracking, BGA took separate bids for the foundations, and while the foundation work was in progress the office completed the design of the superstructure. Bids were then taken for the superstructure, and James McHugh Construction Company became the lead contractor in a joint venture with Brighton Construction Company. McHugh Construction began as a firm specializing in masonry, but it had expanded into heavy construction work, including concrete water-treatment plants and transportation tunnels. It provided expertise in working with curvilinear forms in reinforced concrete and introduced the fiberglass molds for the tower and office structure. McHugh Construction's contract included all the superstructure work–general construction as well as mechanical and electrical services. The firm also filed revisions to the project under its name, and following completion remained responsible for the tenant improvement phase of the building, including the antenna on the west tower and the cast spiral stair in the office building. Leigh Bronson was the general superintendent for McHugh, Norbert Zapinski and Clarence Eckstrom were the project engineers, and Howard Tribble was the finishing superintendent.

Given the fast pace of construction, coordination between trades was essential. In May 1962 the *Chicago Tribune* recorded that communication on-site was made possible only through loudspeakers and telephones: "[the] loudspeaker alerts members of the crew to report to a telephone on every floor… [the] project is a maze of telephone wires including portable head sets."[8] The construction site was also a showcase for union labor. Bronson and Tribble were members of the Cement Masons Union Local 502, one hundred of whose members were involved in constructing the towers, the caissons, and other elements of the project. Members of Cement Masons Union Local 502 and the Laborers International Union of North America (LIUNA) helped put the final batch of concrete into place. Many of the men had arrived from O'Hare Field, as the construction site of O'Hare International Airport was called at that time.[9]

Concrete Structure

Goldberg recognized the importance of centering the team's design effort and constructional ambition on the expression of structure. Self-finished concrete played a key role in this concept because it allowed BGA to explore the potential of curvilinear and circular form and saved 10 to 15 percent of the cost compared to steel. Its use embedded the innovative design in a financially invulnerable phase of the project–once the curvilinear forms of the core and floors of the residential towers were poured in place, these could not be compromised by later budget cuts inevitable in any project.[10] In Marina City engineering thus was the architecture not only for formal and functional reasons but also as a financial strategy. It is even less surprising, given the conceptual centrality of the concrete structure, that McHugh would become the main contractor for the project.

The principles of efficiency and structural, electrical, and mechanical performance were perhaps realized to the greatest extent in the design of the residential towers. The building's circular form had many economies. It offered the highest ratio of usable floor space to exterior skin. It reduced actual wind loads as well as the wind loads needed to be accommodated by building codes. It reduced the length of supply and return runs for utilities. The towers' structural and functional equidistance from the center also eliminated special corner conditions. Poured reinforced concrete and handmade formwork made complex yet structurally efficient forms possible; clever reuse of formwork, lower rebar counts generated by the smoother transfer of horizontal to vertical loads, and careful construction sequencing all generated cost savings. The towers' symmetry was thus a part of their economy of design, engineering, and cost (see Fig. 53).

This focused approach fit perfectly in the tradition of Chicago architecture–which had produced the world's tallest buildings, busiest airports, and deepest tunnels, and even reversed river flows–yet was also deeply personal to Goldberg. Each tower, at 105 feet in diameter, directly expressed its engineering and constructional logic. Each core was 35 feet in diameter and 585 feet high and contained five high-speed elevator shafts (said to be the fastest elevators in the city at the time), two sets of stairways, and all mechanical systems—water distribution, smoke shaft, garbage disposal, fire protection, telephone lines, and the 12,000-volt electrical supply. The cores resisted horizontal wind forces efficiently and helped support the entire tower structure, which was much lighter but just as stable as the equally tall Empire State Building (1931).[11]

Each floor's frame comprised sixteen reinforced concrete beams radiating nearly forty feet from the core trunk toward sixteen exterior columns. The reinforcement cages in the columns, comprising three interlocking spirals, were fabricated to be two to three stories high—the bars passed through and were welded to a three-quarter-inch template for stability and precision of location. Transfer plates, one or two inches thick and ground smooth on both sides, were placed between steel lifts and tack welded to templates, which had holes in the center to allow concrete pours to be continuous and for concrete vibrators to pass through. The transfer of most of the building's wind loads to the central core meant cost savings on the column steelwork—tension splices did not need to be installed between reinforcement cages, and tack welding was sufficient for the template–transfer plate connection. This was possible because the concrete's dead load exceeded the uplift generated by the wind and was transferred to the core by the beams, which acted like heavy tree branches.

The buildings' foundations had to go down into bedrock to prevent the building from settling. Bedrock—the same massive limestone shelf that covers most of the Midwest and reaches as far as Niagara Falls—was located at 110 feet below the surface, and the caissons were drilled a further ten feet into it.[12] Underground water pressure at three separate levels above bedrock meant that the foundation had to be made of a sophisticated system of caissons requiring special drilling and casting techniques. In addition to the weight of water and sand near the surface, the caisson holes had to withstand pressure both from old freight tunnels sixty feet below the surface and from water and silt close to bedrock. Case Foundation Company used a $400,000 caisson drill weighing 125 tons that was capable of drilling to a depth of two hundred feet. The caissons themselves were made as a double steel tube system. A first, larger steel casing was placed to the full depth of the hole, to hold back water and earth. Then a cement caisson was formed in a second, smaller steel casing and was lowered to bedrock. The outside steel casing was then removed. To ease the drilling process, additional water had to be held back with steel sheets, sealing water-filled areas away from the drilling sites. This complex foundations process did not come without problems, some of which affected the construction of the nearby Dearborn Street Bridge. Architectural historian Carl Condit wrote that "water under the Marina City site was in some way released during the sinking of the caisson wells and poured into the wells of the north bridge abutment, resulting in an 18-month delay in the completion of the bridge."[13]

The tower cores rested on the central ring of eight caissons. Cast in concrete using chimneylike construction, the cores rose much faster than the floors themselves, their height and minaret-like proportions forming a spectacular sight from across the river and even from within the Loop. The reusable fiberglass molds ensured a smooth surface and little chance of the formwork getting stuck. BGA had originally designed the cores to be slipformed, but McHugh Construction offered a significant credit if permitted to use the chimneylike construction method.

In a construction spectacle still recalled by Chicagoans today, the towers were built at the amazing speed of one floor per day on alternating towers—or one floor every two days on each tower. [Fig. 49] As the cores were poured, cranes moved up one floor and a construction elevator rose within each shaft to supply building materials. Construction teams moved from one tower to the next, in an alternating rhythm following the concrete's setting time. Each construction sequence (formwork installation, rebar placement, duct installation, concrete pour and surfacing) took one long day. Trucks continuously delivered concrete, and the crane lifted concrete barrels to a specially designed, electrically operated conveyor belt that quickly distributed concrete to the floor pour.

To achieve this construction speed for the residential towers, two special cranes were used. A Linden climbing tower crane, a Danish import, weighing 36,000 pounds, capable of lifting 8,000 pounds at a 95-foot radius, was installed on each tower.[14] [Fig. 50] In a prior project Goldberg had seen the capacity of such cranes vastly improve construction speed.[15] The crane bases were placed about three levels below that of the work itself, close to the core's center, with their load spread to a further four floors below by temporary shoring. They were hydraulically lifted to follow the construction—one floor a day. The cranes became a powerful image on the Chicago skyline and so entered the popular consciousness; later, rumors abounded that they were to be used to help hoist large furniture into apartments on move-in day.[16]

The concrete pour process began every morning at 5:30 AM, when workers raised the Linden crane. At 6:00 AM carpenters stripped the forms from the core poured the previous day. [Fig. 51] By 7:00 the crane was in its new position, allowing the core forms to be raised and carpenters to place door and utility openings. The ironworkers followed, placing reinforcing steel bars—two rings of vertical bars of varying sizes and horizontal temperature bars, with sizes decreasing higher up the building. By noon the carpenters began to work on raising the interior forms, which were normally ready for pouring by 2:30 PM. The crane lifted everything: forms, box-outs for door and duct openings, reinforcing steel, and concrete. By 8:00 PM all the concreting was complete.[17] The Portland Cement Association, whose offices were three blocks away and who contributed a concrete engineer to the project at no cost, documented the construction process in a promotional film that recorded the fast but steady pace with which the towers were constructed.

Another innovation, initiated by McHugh Construction, was the use of reinforcing mesh for the construction of the parking ramps and apartment floors. Although these had originally been designed with normal reinforcing steel in mind, the contractor requested, and was permitted, to change this to electrically welded wire mesh, just coming to the marketplace. This was another important factor in speeding up construction, as it meant less time to set and tie the mesh, more accuracy in its placement, and greater stability of position during the concrete pour itself.

Speed and economy were also achieved through the use of polyester resin fiberglass molds for the walls, columns, beams, and slabs. [Fig. 52] Manufactured by Engineered Concrete Forms of Chicago, they were reinforced with steel and wood. The core forms' width of thirteen feet followed the core's arc and the building's floor-to-floor height. Although they were expensive (four to five dollars per square foot at the time) and heavy (5,200 pounds each) they were reused sixty-seven times. Their external steel and wood reinforcement

49. Construction site with spectators,
Marina City (1959–1967), Bertrand
Goldberg Associates, Chicago, IL,
ca. 1961.

50. Tower core rising with Linden Crane,
Marina City (1959–1967), Bertrand
Goldberg Associates, Chicago, IL, 1962.
Photograph. Bertrand Goldberg Archive, Ryerson
and Burnham Archives, The Art Institute of Chicago.
© The Art Institute of Chicago.

51. Concrete work, Marina City (1959–
1967), Bertrand Goldberg Associates,
Chicago, IL. Portland Cement Association
[photograph]. Bertrand Goldberg Archive, Ryerson
and Burnham Archives, The Art Institute of Chicago.
© The Art Institute of Chicago.

52. Concrete molds laid on the ground, Marina City (1959–1967), Bertrand Goldberg Associates, Chicago, IL. Portland Cement Association [photograph]. Bertrand Goldberg Archive, Ryerson and Burnham Archives, The Art Institute of Chicago. © The Art Institute of Chicago.

made them self-stabilizing and therefore they needed no through-the-wall form ties or spreaders. The beam fiberglass forms were reinforced by framed timber U-shores with ledges and clips on the side to support the floor formwork. The slab forms were precast fiberglass and cost only a quarter as much as the core forms because they had no steel or wood reinforcement. Instead they rested on a flat of two-by-fours at six-inch centers, which were themselves made into seventy-five-square-foot units. A secondary, transverse structure of four-by-eights ran from beam to beam, with intermediate four-by-four supports. The column formwork was also fiberglass and came in four sections—two short and two long pieces. L-shaped pieces were used for the interior columns and half-diamond pieces were used for the exterior ones. Steel reinforcement along the long sides strengthened the molds and provided seating for bolts connecting the molds together for the pour; timber stiffeners provided additional stability. At the top of the long sections the forms fanned out to connect column to beam. The short sections at the column's base provided a two-foot-high cleanout section. Only three complete sets of column-, beam-, and floor-forms were used in each tower—this allowed for their removal after five to six days, when the concrete had hardened sufficiently. Reshoring provided support while the concrete hardened to three thousand pounds per square inch or more. Apart from its speed and ease of assembly, the smoothness of the fiberglass formwork saved time and money by avoiding finishing work, allowing for paint to be applied directly to concrete internally and a concrete self-finish to be shown externally.

The concrete mix comprised two types: regular aggregate concrete, delivered from a nearby central mix plant, was used for the exterior and interior walls, and lightweight, expanded shale aggregate concrete was used for the interior floors. The floors exposed to the exterior (parking ramps and balconies) were poured using a stronger, six-bag mix for durability. An ingenious system of conveyor belts distributed concrete from the hopper to several floor pours

53. Office building vaults and promenade deck, Marina City (1959–1967), Bertrand Goldberg Associates, Chicago, IL.
Orlando Cabanban [photographer]. Bertrand Goldberg Archive, Ryerson and Burnham Archives, The Art Institute of Chicago. Digital File # 200203.081229-318
© The Art Institute of Chicago.

at the same time, powered by a synchronous electric motor, which allowed all conveyor belt motors to start and stop at the same time. The lightweight concrete used for internal floors did have some disadvantages—in low winter temperatures pouring had to stop. Nevertheless, a new floor—twelve-thousand square feet—was completed per tower on alternating days, except during cold weather.[18] Carpenters worked around the clock to form the new floor and beam formwork once it had been lifted to the new level by the Linden crane. Once the formwork was struck, the slab was leveled and floated with long-handled floats. On the parking ramps, the finish was left rough to resist skidding.

After the concrete hardened, the tower crane lifted itself up on the newly cast form, raised the molds, and the process was repeated. The two towers followed alternate cycles of pouring—a clever way to ensure that the concrete and carpentry crews were doing the same work every day. In late 1961, 250 men were working daily on the site to make this possible.[19]

The concrete beams were poured using both regular and lightweight concrete. Regular strength concrete in columns and beams was necessary to prevent spalling when the fiberglass molds were removed; in the beams it was only used for a two-inch bottom layer, with lightweight concrete filling the remainder. The use of lightweight concrete allowed for a floor-to-floor height of eight feet six inches and smaller dimensions for the structural frame. This in turn led to savings that more than compensated for the delays due to pour stoppages on very cold days.

The concrete's strength in the columns decreased as the building rose, but for the core, which had to reach 2,200 pounds per square inch (psi) in twenty hours to support the pours above, 5,000 psi ready-mix concrete was used throughout its height. The amount of concrete reduced as the core got higher: at the top the core walls were only twelve inches, whereas at the bottom they were thirty inches thick. The conveyors for the concrete pours too were lifted each day by the Linden crane. Once the crane reached the core's top, with concrete pouring completed, it was dismantled and taken down in the elevator.[20] The spiral concrete garage floors were much easier and faster to pour than the residential floors because of the relatively small presence of mechanical and electrical trades and therefore the lesser need for coordination.[21]

The office building structural system was a reinforced concrete frame. The exterior facade was made of cast-in-place concrete mullions that included delicate rabbets in order to receive the glass directly—a clever use of window frames as structural members.[22] A series of trapezoidal concrete columns, which coordinated with the post-and-beam structural system below the plaza, passed through the bowling alley's enclosure and terminated in a soaring series of groin vaults supporting the office block. [Fig. 53] This created another story above the promenade at the top of the bowling alley element—an extraordinary cathedral-like. The columns and vaults were poured using fiberglass forms similar to those used in the towers. At the top of the arches forming the groin vaults' vertical exterior facade, imperfections in curvature (most likely resulting from the inability to form a complex curve in the fiberglass mold) show the mold maker's and concrete operator's handwork. The office building's structure above the vaults was also ingenious. Externally supported by tightly spaced in situ concrete mullions, the internal load was carried by a set of central columns. The use of fiberglass molds for the mullions allowed for a high level of accuracy, maintaining low tolerances for the slot that was to receive frameless glass.

Steel Structure

The theater was the one exception to the dominance of concrete as a structural material. Its original structure was to consist of catenary steel cables suspended from a reinforced concrete compression ring supported at two points. The cables were to be covered with sprayed-on concrete to form the roof enclosure and fireproofing. However, this proved too ambitious and expensive and was revised, with the saddle shape constructed using regular steel beams and triangulated smaller members completing the complex form and providing structural stability. The theater's base was supported by columns set back from the exterior, wrapped in single-pane, three-quarter-inch-thick glazed curved glass.

As the theatre building's roof profile changed to the saddle shape, other transformations occurred. The roof's steel arches pivoted along the roofline's length, perpendicular to the catenary. The materials, originally shingle on masonry, changed to lead on a sprayed concrete roof on top of the steel frame. [Fig. 54]

The theater also became the first-ever building to be fully clad in lead.[23] Lead was used because of its capacity to sheathe the complex form, to accommodate the movement anticipated in the theater roof's structure, and because of its sound-deadening qualities. Its gray color was also a suitable counterpoint to the concrete of the towers and office building, and its ability to absorb sound meant that it also symbolized the building's internal function. Traditional standing seams were used, horizontally on the roof and vertically on the walls, with the locks rolled in the direction of the slope. To avoid flat surfaces buckling at seam locations where a number of lead sheets overlapped, the sheets were fabricated to be tapered on one side. Wastage of lead only amounted to 1 percent.[24]

Although the theater roof structure ended up much bulkier than the original curvature seen in early drawings, the building still possessed an unusually organic quality. Carl Condit admired its structure and location within the

54. Theater structure, Marina City (1959–1967), Bertrand Goldberg Associates, Chicago, IL, ca. 1965. Ed Center, Bertrand Goldberg Associates [photographer]. Bertrand Goldberg Archive, Ryerson and Burnham Archives, The Art Institute of Chicago. Digital File #200203.081229-295 © The Art Institute of Chicago.

complex: "[The theater building] is all hidden away, but perfectly at home in the staggering exhibition of structural virtuosity embodied in Marina City."[25] [Fig. 55]

Finishes and Environmental Services

The thorough logic that drove BGA's treatment of structural materials and systems, as well as construction sequencing, extended into interior finishes. These included concrete, steel, and glass, among other materials. [Fig. 56] The apartments featured thermopane windows, which were set back behind the floor overhang in order to minimize heat gain and loss. The office glazing was set directly into the load-bearing concrete mullions. [Fig. 57] The use of mullion-free curved glass for the theater entrance was exquisitely handled; the ability of the glass to last for decades at the end of a sizable cantilever without any damage is evidence of BGA's capable detailing.

The concrete was self-finished but was painted on the interior. The lath interior partitions were also painted, but problems with their finishes persisted throughout the project and led to lawsuits following the project's completion. Within the apartments the bathrooms featured floor-to-ceiling glass tiles, while kitchens had a Marina City–inspired wall paper. Built-in cabinets in the dressing areas were made of molded plastic, with stainless steel and chrome used for the mirrored cabinets. BGA's female architects, in a division of labor typical of the time, were assigned to work with the first tenants to allow them to choose finishes for the apartments, offices, and retail spaces. Goldberg himself evolved a color palette and lighting scheme for the tower corridors, emphasizing the importance of low lighting to create a sense of comfort and enclosure. The entrances to each apartments featured asphalt tile floors, while all semipublic lobby spaces were carpeted.

The office interiors received particular attention, as they were intended to be customized for individual tenants—not only in terms of finishes but also in plan layouts. BGA worked closely with tenants during the tenant improvement phase of the project, developing not only office layouts but also the design of many, although not all, spaces below the office floors and within the commercial platform.

Goldberg's concern with comfort and efficiency extended to careful consideration of environmental systems. Marina City fully utilized natural light and heat gain and loss; the balconies' ten-foot overhang was designed to create shade during the summer.[26] The petal-shaped apartments had service areas grouped close to the core while the living areas opened up centrifugally to the cityscape, offering only one facade to the exterior, resulting in lower heating and cooling costs. However, in terms of heating, cooling, and ventilation, Marina City also drew on the latest technology; it was a fully electric building and, at the time of its completion, had the country's second-largest nonindustrial electrical system, exceeded only by the Pentagon. It was the first all-electric apartment building.[27] All-electric living embodied the spirit of the newly mechanized domestic space of the 1950s; it was clean, quiet, and easily controllable.

Electricity for the complex was provided by a transmission substation about two thirds of a mile from the site, supplying electricity to the building's main switchroom through underground cables, each connected to a separate bus at the substation. The switchroom was to prevent a power outage in the towers, if cable failure occurred in the street, by switching from one cable to another. From the switchroom, each of the tower cores was supplied with a

←

55. Construction workers on theater roof structure, Marina City (1959–1967), Bertrand Goldberg Associates, Chicago, IL, ca. 1965. Ed Center, Bertrand Goldberg Associates [photographer]. Bertrand Goldberg Archive, Ryerson and Burnham Archives, The Art Institute of Chicago. Digital File #200203.081229-297 © The Art Institute of Chicago.

overleaf, p. 84 →
56. Tower structural plan, parking level, Marina City (1959–1967), Severud Associates Consulting Engineers, Chicago, IL, 1962.

overleaf, p. 85 → →
57. Mullion detail, office building, Marina City (1959–1967), Bertrand Goldberg Associates, Chicago, IL, 1962. Bertrand Goldberg Archive, Architecture and Design Department, Art Institute of Chicago

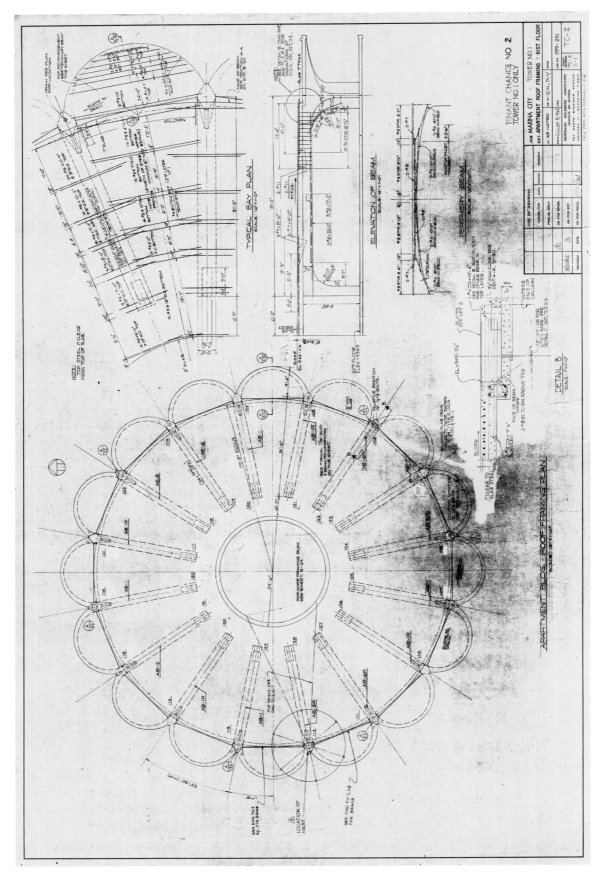

84

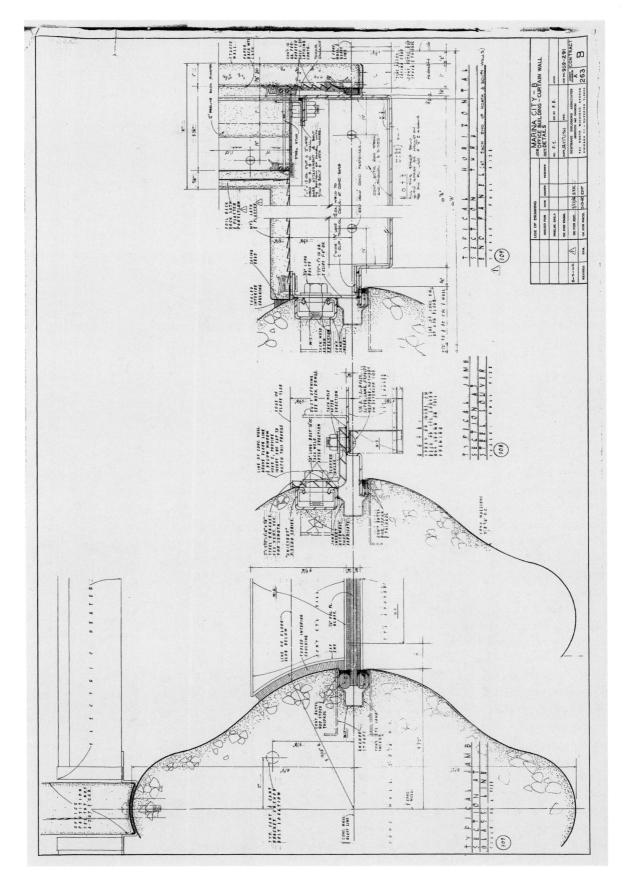

12,000-volt electrical transmission line feeding two different electrical vaults: the community vaults that supplied the apartments and the service vaults that supplied the elevators and corridor lighting and heating, the laundry, and other shared services. The community vaults were located within the the core elevator corridor on even-numbered floors and were packed very efficiently into their small space. A full-scale model to study the heat generated in such a confined space and to test the configuration of the cables and transformers was built, with live supply under actual load conditions, at the Commonwealth Edison Company Technical Center.[28] The building service vaults were located in the towers' base and on the ninteenth, twentieth, fifty-ninth, and sixtieth floors. The two largest basement vaults providing most of the electrical supply for the public areas' heating and lighting, as well as for the bowling alley, restaurant, and theater, among others, were located below the boat storage area floor. Subject to flooding, these vaults employed submersible equipment—an ingenious solution to "the problems of 'bigness'"—the production, distribution, and sale of electricity on a scale that had never been known before.[29]

Each apartment had tenant controls for electrical heating and ventilation, electrical ranges, hot water heaters, and waste-disposal units—a democratic concept for its time.[30] Electric radiant heating under the apartment windows was the main source of heat, supplemented with a unit above each balcony door acting as a heat booster in winter or as an air-conditioning unit in the summer. The limited heat output was possible because the apartments effectively had only one external wall and also benefited from some heat gain during the winter months, for all but the north-facing apartments, through the floor-to-ceiling sealed double-glazed external walls. Apartments also made their own hot water, with the early use of forty-gallon fast-recovery water heaters. The use of electricity for local water and air heating saved money by eliminating space that would have been taken up by ductwork.[31] Each apartment also had a master TV antenna, a telephone connection, and an electric door annunciator.

The lighting was designed by BGA—in keeping with the building concept, wall and ceiling lights were circular in form. The building also had more electrical outlets than was typical at the time, with twenty-four circuits for a two-bedroom apartment.[32] The General Electric kitchen provided the Americana double-oven range as standard. The shared laundry lounge included electric automatic washers and dryers.

In the office building electrical systems were also used inventively; all-electric lighting, heating, and cooling systems were fully controlled by its tenants, offering tremendous flexibility. The heat generated from lighting was recirculated to reduce the cost of heating through Chicago's long winter. In the summer months, the excess heat from the lamps was dissipated into the exhaust system, thus making less work for the office air-conditioning system. The lighting, providing 250-foot candles at desk level, was carefully designed to provide the highest level of comfort and productivity; the ceiling was also the supply and return air grille system for the air handling.

Nevertheless, in the office building, not all design decisions were intended to save energy—rather, they celebrated the power of electricity to solve problems, including those of heat loss. The office building's floor, raised above the podium slab as a formal rather than functional gesture, was heated with electrical coils to counteract heat loss. The swimming pool set alongside external walls in the podium was provided with ceiling-mounted infrared heating units to compensate for the same problem, and the floors around the pool were similarly heated with electrical power. In the residential towers the parking ramps' first two spirals were heated to melt snow and ice, as were the external surfaces of the podium and the apartment balconies. Electricity was also a feature in the theater building—as planned, but not built, almost every seat was to be provided with its own light source.

The towers had the fastest electrically operated elevators in the city at that time—the fully automatic Otis Autotronic electronic high-speed elevators moved at seven hundred feet per minute. Such design choices were intended to project the image of progressive living—and to save more than two million dollars in capital costs. In addition to the savings in space, the use of electricity saved the cost of a hot water riser system, and the twelve kilovolt risers in the core reduced the size and quantity of electrical conduit in the apartment buildings.[33]

The management of airflow was also carefully considered. Air in the towers' core was under positive pressure to prevent smells being drawn out of the apartments and into the corridors. Instead, air passed from the core to the apartments, and it was extracted through kitchen and bathroom exhausts to the outside. [Fig. 58] The core air was maintained at a temperature compatible with the apartments through heat pumps and air handling equipment on the roof.[34] In keeping with Goldberg's pursuit of a complex using no combustible fuels, even paper and similar materials were to be trucked away to avoid incineration on-site. Pumped air at the bottom of the boat slips was used in the winter to break up the ice and thus prevent damage to boats, and telephone poles were anchored by chains located at the marina's front to prevent pack ice from entering the dock bays.[35]

Hand and Machine

Despite the dominance of repetitive construction processes, there were many examples in the detail design and construction of Marina City where mass production met the human hand. The groin vault supporting the office building is one example—showing an uneven concrete surface resulting from a manually created mold; the theater building's lead roof is another. The fiberglass molds used for parts of the project were another.[36] The rebar placed within the fiberglass mold, with the exception of the horizontal mesh placed within the floors, was bent on-site; although this was done by machine, the final placement of the curved elements still required careful coordination. The thinness and elegance of the office building's concrete mullions, and the insertion of glass without the need for intermediate steel or aluminum mullions, would not have been possible without the fiberglass molds.

Another example of the hand meeting the machine, involving the careful laying of ductwork within rebar cages, was the exhaust ducts' location for each unit, as well as soil pipes in the concrete beams of the towers. The integration of air flow and waste systems with structure prevented awkward duct pathways, maintained clear internal surfaces, and reduced average ceiling heights—a true unity of structure and building systems.

The complex's curvilinear forms also involved the hand and the machine. A box of French curves was used to geometrically extract the theater's sections and elevations, the residential tower's sections, and groin vault drawings from the plan and the elevations. Wherever systems did not elegantly integrate with one another, improvised solutions were introduced. For example, in order to increase the number of boats in the wet dock, the architects revised the marina plan. As a result, the garbage chute in one of the towers ended above water

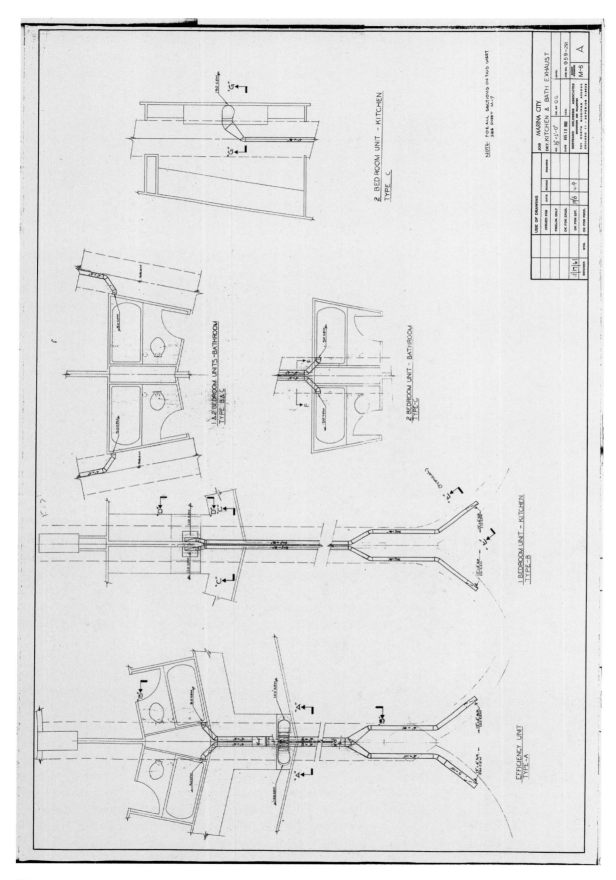

2 BEDROOM UNIT - KITCHEN
TYPE C

1 & 2 BEDROOM UNITS - BATHROOM
TYPE B & C

2 BEDROOM UNIT - BATHROOM
TYPE C

1 BEDROOM UNIT - KITCHEN
TYPE B

EFFICIENCY UNIT
TYPE A

NOTE: FOR ALL SECTIONS ON THIS SHEET
SEE SHEET M-7

JOB MARINA CITY
DET. KITCHEN & BATH EXHAUST
NO. ½"=1'-0"   DWN.
DATE DEC 18 1962   CORR.
DR BY O.G.   JOB NO. 959-291
SHEET M-6

BERTRAND GOLDBERG ASSOCIATES
ARCHITECTS AND ENGINEERS
321 NORTH MICHIGAN AVENUE
CHICAGO 11 · SUPERIOR 7-8825

USE OF DRAWING
ISSUED FOR | DATE | SIGNED
PRELIM. ONLY
OK FOR ENGR.
OK FOR EST.
OK FOR PROD.
SYM. | REVISED
A

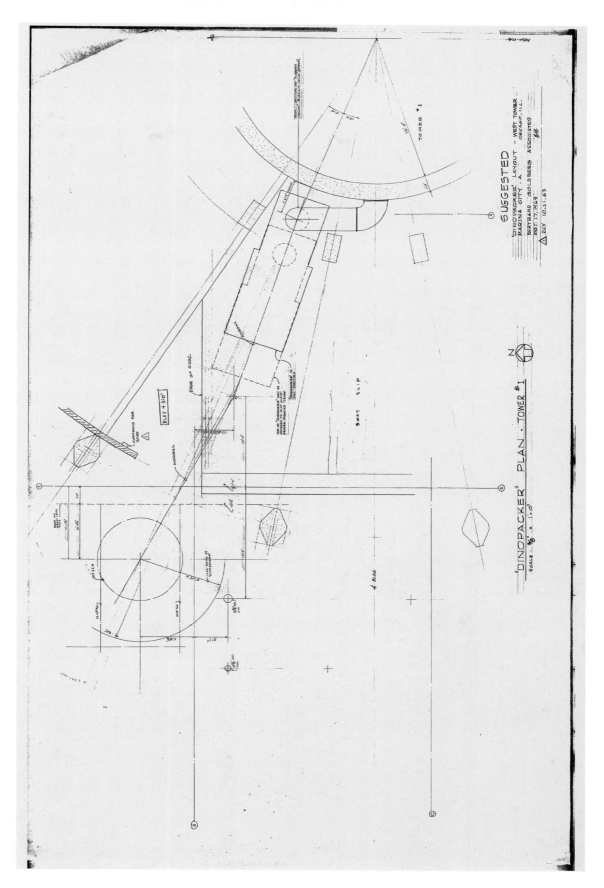

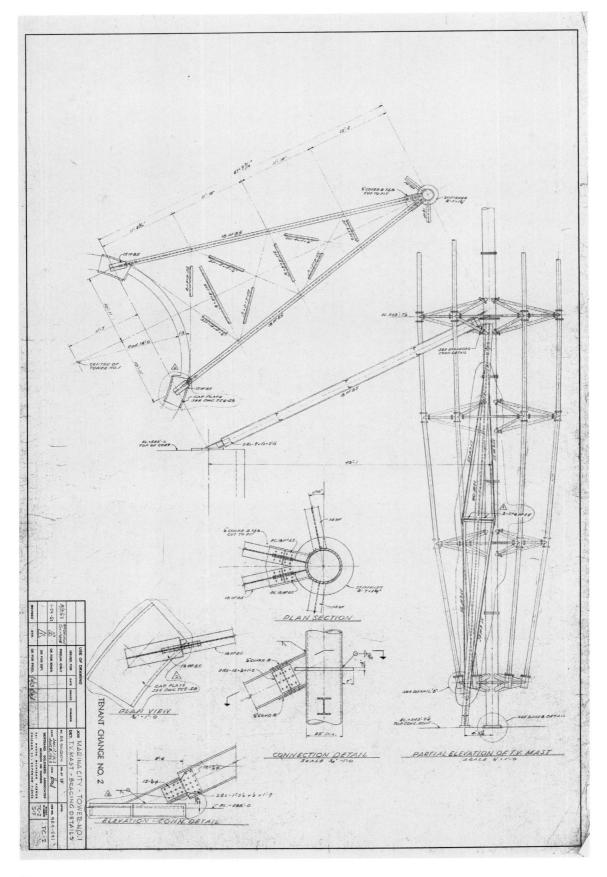

PLAN SECTION

PLAN VIEW

CONNECTION DETAIL
SCALE ⅜" = 1'-0

PARTIAL ELEVATION OF T.V. MAST
SCALE ¼" = 1'-0

ELEVATION - CONN. DETAIL

instead of land. This was resolved by suspending a dumpster above the water from rails mounted on the ceiling. The dumpster then rolled along the rails, turned, and was collected by a dumpster truck on land. [**Fig. 59**]

Finally, with a dramatic flourish, technology was turned into functional art at the building's roofline. The top of the west tower had a tall TV antenna, designed in collaboration with Severud's office—a tall metal structure, whose constructivist aesthetic boldly contrasted with the plasticity of the concrete forms below. [**Fig. 60**] Lights were installed on the antenna, as a part of the tenant improvements phase of the project, to predict the weather. Lights traveled up the antenna to indicate an anticipated rise in temperature; they traveled down the antenna to indicate a commensurate fall. No change in lighting pattern meant that the weather would remain the same. Flashing lights indicated rain or snow, and rapidly flashing lights an impending storm. The lighting was even to be used to announce sports results, such as home team victories, using different light signals.[37]

Marina City's construction was not, however, without tragedy—three carpenters were killed on September 15, 1961, when scaffolding collapsed after a foreman loosened a support; later a laborer was killed falling off a balcony. In addition, at least six workers were injured during construction.[38] Lawsuits resulting from the deaths and injuries of these individuals led to revisions in Chicago building codes relating to elevators and safety harnesses; these improvements in fact saved the lives of the six injured Marina City operatives in 1962.[39]

Despite these problems, Marina City's structural ambition was impressive, particularly given that BGA had undertaken no previous projects at that scale. It was perhaps this lack of experience that gave the office the courage to tame industrial production with a delicate hand. This merger of mechanistic and manual fabrications was also largely driven by savings and finance—another important arena of Goldberg's work that included both the negotiating table and the construction site.

61. Aerial view of Chicago River looking west, Marina City centered, Marina City (1959–1967), Bertrand Goldberg Associates, Chicago, IL. Hedrich-Blessing [photographer], SN-800-02, Chicago History Museum.

chapter four

the deal

CURRENT AMERICAN ARCHITECTURE IS NOT A MATTER OF
ART, BUT OF BUSINESS. A BUILDING MUST PAY OR THERE
WILL BE NO INVESTOR READY WITH THE MONEY TO MEET
ITS COST. THIS IS AT ONCE THE CURSE AND THE GLORY OF
AMERICAN ARCHITECTURE.

—BARR FERREE, AIA NATIONAL CONVENTION, CHICAGO, 1893

Marina City was the largest financial partnership between federal, union, banking, and business interests ever seen in a housing complex on the American
continent. In Marina City, labor unions, the political machine of Chicago, the
federal government, real estate interests, bankers, and architects used the market economy's mechanisms to advance new ideals about urban life. In particular
the project was the result of astute financial know-how possessed by William
McFetridge, Chuck Swibel, and Bertrand Goldberg. Goldberg had previously
been exposed to some of the financial and political systems needed to realize the project, and he expanded his knowledge to drive his architectural and
social vision of the building as the project developed. The efficiently designed
complex was built for ten to twelve dollars a square foot; however, its cost also
was low because "cheaper" money funded the project. Innovative manipulation
of Chicago planning and zoning regulations and FHA rules made the mixed-use
program economically viable, Marina City's residential mortgage insurable, and
the entire project attractive to its investing partners. In *Chicago Architecture:
1940–1970* Carl Condit suggested that McFetridge and Swibel struggled to
find conventional funding because banks were reluctant to fund a project with
such radical programming and form.[1] Janitors' Union documents, however, suggest that the idea of mixed-use and FHA insurance emerged very early in the
project.[2] Any difficulty in finding backers was thus due as much to the project's
scale as to Marina City's architectural and urban novelty.

    According to Goldberg, it was some time after completing the Janitors'
Union's offices on West Randolph Street that McFetridge floated the idea that
led to Marina City. Goldberg was interested in the challenge. His work on

Standard Houses and the Drexel Boulevard Town and Garden Apartments had exposed him to public financing in private funding contexts; Standard Houses had also provided him with experience in negotiating residential mortgage insurance with the FHA. Finally, through his work with prefabrication he had learned—albeit at a much smaller scale—how to deliver efficient and affordable design.

McFetridge, Swibel, and Goldberg were all aware of the market need for residential space in downtown Chicago. In April 1959 a *Chicago Market Analysis Report* prepared by the Real Estate Research Corporation of Chicago for the Chicago Central Area Committee argued that the city needed 39,000 new housing units of all types in its downtown, including ten-thousand units in the $125 to $250 per month bracket for efficiency, one-, and two-bedroom apartments. The report suggested that demand for suburban single-family dwellings had peaked, with 40 percent of all renters working downtown wishing to live there and that demand for downtown living could be as high as 47,000 dwellings.[3] It also showed that one out of every four married couples without children and two-person families working downtown wanted to live in the Chicago central area—a need for 5,600 downtown dwellings. It reported that 23 percent of the downtown dwelling market consisted of single persons or two unrelated persons living together—yet another 4,200 dwellings. Finally, it stated that one out of every five three-person families wanted to live downtown—another 2,900 dwellings. Most importantly, the report identified 52,000 persons as employed within a half-mile radius of Marina City, with 80 percent of lakeshore land for apartment building that had been available at the end of World War II now occupied.[4] Other research by the national American Committee to Improve Our Neighborhoods (ACTION) had also shown an increased demand for downtown living.[5] An earlier 1958 Chicago Central Area Committee report had designated the future site of Marina City as part of the Central Area Development Plan (1958); the ensuing Chicago zoning ordinance identified offices, apartments, hotels, or institutional structures as permitted development.[6]

These reports resonated with Mayor Richard J. Daley's desire to revive central Chicago. Although Marina City came early in his administration, Daley, unlike his counterparts in many other cities, invested in Chicago's downtown. His vision rightly recognized the city's past and future success as a hub of human, material, and transportation infrastructures. Yet construction costs were higher due to the depth of bedrock and zoning regulations, and wages were higher due to Chicago's powerful unions, making development less dense and more expensive.[7] Nevertheless, when a 3.1-acre site in downtown Chicago owned by the Chicago and North Western Railway became available in August 1959, McFetridge presented the Marina City idea to the Janitors' Union's executive board. According to Goldberg, it was Swibel who saw the potential to switch union investments from government or government-insured securities to National Housing Act Title VII—insured mortgages.[8]

At the Janitors' Union executive board meeting McFetridge argued that people preferred to live near their places of employment and therefore Marina City would attract renters. This would make an excellent investment for the union and a place for its members to work. McFetridge also argued that investment in Marina City would help reverse the deterioration of land values in central Chicago—so profiting the union and the city:

We feel we are making a sound investment of union funds that must be held in trust....We believe in Chicago; we believe that an investment in the future of the downtown is one of the soundest investments that can be made.[9]

Marina City was to be no utopian project. McFetridge is reported to have told Goldberg "I don't want socialist housing...I want to create patterns that can be followed by private capital."[10] Goldberg's response was clear: "I was faced with a mandate from Bill McFetridge to show people that it is more pleasant to live in the city and less expensive."[11] While McFetridge and Swibel drove the project's financial and political aspects, Goldberg provided important additional skills: establishing and adapting a marketable program, making presentations to funders, pursuing maximum design and construction efficiencies, and managing much of the project's publicity.

His 24–7 concept of "living above the store" was not only an urban ideal but also made financial sense. Goldberg presented the financial argument for mixed-use development:

No city can afford this specialization—both in terms of the tax burden and the terrific cost of idle facilities—police, water, gas, electricity, fire department. This is a one-shift city. Marina City will be a two-shift city. Without both a daytime and nighttime population, the cost of recreation, garage, rents, [and] taxes would all be higher. There is no working unit—business, recreational, residential, service—which by itself can stand the high cost of the central city.[12]

Goldberg also brought urban and architectural skills to the project—he helped McFetridge and Swibel select the riverfront site:

I said to Bill McFetridge, "You asked me to find you a piece of property. We have nine pieces of property, eight of which are within the budget that you suggested to me, and the ninth of which is too rich for your blood." He said, "What one was that?" I said, "We can walk out of Fritzel's here and I'll show it to you," and we did. The three of us stood out there on the sidewalk and I said, "There." He looked at it, and he said to Chuck Swibel, "See what you can buy it for."[13]

Swibel acquired an option on the land sometime before the middle of August 1959.[14] This meant that the Janitors' Union did not have to pay a down payment on the land until it had the funds for the project; Goldberg, McFetridge, and Swibel spent the next four months establishing the project's financial viability.

The site's sale prospectus waxed lyrical about its potential, claiming: "In the years ahead, the river will be to Chicago what the Thames is to London; the Tiber to Rome; the Seine to Paris; or the Guadalquivir to Seville—a vital part of the city's life and a prominent feature of its many downtown attractions."[15] In August 1959 the Chicago Planning Department confirmed the viability of development on the site, and at the beginning of September the FHA confirmed that it would consider the funding strategy proposal. Assured by this support, the Janitors' Union's executive board in September 1959 authorized McFetridge to commission a feasibility study and release news of the project. McFetridge proudly addressed his members: "Our union, which has always serviced the

62. North Marina City Corporation share, 1959.

city with labor, will now service the city with capital investment and planning. We want to show the way for other investors with capital."[16]

In October 1959 two separate companies—the Marina City Building Corporation (MCBC) and North Marina City Building Corporation (NMCBC), responsible respectively for the residential towers and the rest of the complex— were established, with McFetridge as president, Ernest Anderson of Local 1 as secretary, and Thomas J. Burke of Local 25 as treasurer. Local 1 and Local 25 were both Chicago branches of the Janitors' Union; Chicago was thus effectively in charge of both corporations. In addition, one month later McFetridge insisted that he should hold all the stock issued for the benefit of the sponsoring unions. He nevertheless agreed for the other sponsors to be represented on the board of directors—a verbal commitment that would haunt him later.[17] Shares in both corporations were issued to the stakeholders even though the project's financing was not yet completed. [Fig. 62]

In December 1959 the Janitors' Union paid the down payment for the land.[18] The sale offered the title to the land around and between as well as the air rights over the railroad tracks.[19] As Goldberg later reported, Swibel had negotiated a significant discount in the purchase price: "The asking price was $3,700,000 but after weeks of work, 'and a couple of pints of blood' Swibel wangled an option at a reduced price of $2,500,000."[20] For real estate tax purposes the land was separated into two divisions that mirrored the project's financial and management division into the two corporations.[21] The union had committed itself to a total of 135,000 square feet at $18.50 per square foot in the largest single private land transaction in the history of metropolitan Chicago.[22]

63. Marina City preconstruction event, David Sullivan, Lester Asher, William McFetridge, and Bertrand Goldberg at the Astor Hotel, New York City, 1960.
Merkle Press Inc. [photograph]. By permission of Pubco Corporation. Bertrand Goldberg Archive, Ryerson and Burnham Archives, The Art Institute of Chicago. © The Art Institute of Chicago.

Despite, or perhaps because of the heroic scale of the project, Goldberg was enlisted to persuade the Janitors' Union membership of the project's value. The large-scale model of Marina City traveled to New York for the Janitors' Union's annual convention in May 1960, at which McFetridge was replaced as president by his protégé and soon-to-be nemesis David Sullivan, and where conventioneers, including major national figures in labor and politics, endorsed the project. Goldberg actively participated in these marketing and fundraising events and is often shown in photographs with McFetridge, Swibel, and Sullivan, advocating for the projects in various public events. [Fig. 63]

Political Will

To be financially viable the proposal had to overcome two critical obstacles that could only be removed through major legislative change. The Chicago zoning code had to permit mixed-use development and the federal mortgage insurance must be available for downtown apartments. Neither was the case; Goldberg played a major role in changing this status quo.

The Chicago zoning code was based on single-use categories for individual lots. Marina City's mixed-use program was thus prohibited. Federal mortgage insurance was critical because it guaranteed to commercial lenders that once the residential towers were completed and construction loans paid off, the mortgage would—in case of default—be paid by the federal government. The Janitors' Union would still have to find a bank to fund the actual residential mortgage, but that bank would be guaranteed the repayment of its loan. This made investment safer for a private lender and therefore lowered the mortgage's cost—in effect creating "cheaper money" that could in turn help lower rents—or increase return on investment if the savings were not passed on to tenants.

However, federal mortgage insurance was only available for suburban family housing. Addressing these two challenges required local and national negotiations; the full purchase price for the land would not be paid by the Janitors' Union until this code was changed. This was how Swibel got his "option" on the land without "paying"; now Goldberg was needed to complete the deal.

The first problem—that of the Chicago zoning code—was solved locally, simply and ingeniously. Goldberg and Swibel worked closely with Ira Bach in the City of Chicago's Department of Planning and Development (who had long-standing links to the union movement) to reclassify the land as an entire mixed-use *district*, thus cleverly bringing the site into conformity with the code without having to change it.[23] The project became a planned urban development, the first in Chicago.

The second problem took longer to resolve. McFetridge, Swibel, and Goldberg worked with the FHA's offices in Chicago and Washington, D.C., to reclassify married couples without children, and single individuals, as a family, the eligible unit for federal housing mortgages. John Waner, the new director of Chicago's FHA Insuring Office, was a key player in this process. In February 1960, Waner stated:

> The $36 million dollar [sic] is to be insured under FHA Title 7. Title 7 is a new kind of insurance concept made available by Congress. In the processing of this project, the local FHA office and the central office in Washington will take the same bold and imaginative approach that was used when Congress first gave to the American people the long term, low down-payment mortgage insurance program in 1934.[24]

However, it soon became clear that the Janitors' Union would get mortgage insurance only under Title II, Section 207 of the 1934 National Housing Act, and thus the government would insure only 90 percent of the mortgaged amount.[25] The Union had to find investors willing to accept the additional risk.[26]

In June 1960 Julian Zimmerman, FHA federal commissioner, confirmed that the FHA would guarantee Marina City's residential mortgage component.[27] At the ceremony celebrating this decision, Waner, referring to the modern movement in architecture launched with the Chicago School, lauded Goldberg as joining its other famous members.[28] A press release from the Goldberg office proudly proclaimed the "deal" as another set of Marina City "firsts"—not only the first FHA-insured downtown housing but also the biggest housing mortgage insurance the FHA had ever issued.[29]

This single but radical reorientation of federal housing policy made the housing component of the complex financially viable for both the Janitors' Union and private investors. Zimmerman was credited with much of the leadership in stemming the flow of populations from downtowns into the suburbs, but the decision was also the result of the Chicago political machine's national influence and the advocacy of the project partners, including Goldberg.[30]

Goldberg traveled to Washington, D.C., several times between August 1959 and February 1960 to present a conservative proposal comprising two square residential towers and argue for FHA regulations change. He felt that a more familiar square form would make a policy shift in Washington easier. Once back in Chicago the tower design was changed back to its circular form. Goldberg also drew on his real estate experience to move the project across a funding hurdle:

> I got an approval for a certain amount of money, but it was a million dollars shy of what we needed. We had only until the next day at noon to get FHA approval. I went to John Waner....He thought the Marina City idea was just great....I said, "...I either have your approval for another million dollars by twelve o'clock or the project is dead. John, analyzing that million dollars against the whole transaction amounts to the fact that you have to increase the rental income of each room in this project by fifty cents a month. John, is your judgment so accurate that you think you could not get fifty cents a month for each room as an increase in our rental income?"...I had done my homework. John called in his chief underwriter....The two of them looked at me and said "We'll give you the fifty cents a month."[31]

Goldberg believed that progressive architectural ideas would be accepted in a consumer democracy only if they were more affordable than traditional solutions—affordability made radical design possible. His Harvard and Bauhaus experience taught him about the link between culture, economics, and politics. Yet at the Bauhaus he also experienced the German anti-Modernist backlash and understood the need for new social and architectural ideals to be integrated within, rather than be placed in opposition to, market-driven capitalism.

Private Investment

Marina City was first and foremost intended as an investment opportunity for the Janitors' Union, who became its first but not largest stakeholder. In 1959 it committed $1.1 million for the project; in addition Local 1 pledged one million dollars, Local 32B half a million dollars, and the Building Service Employees

Pension Trust (West Coast) another half a million dollars, to total $3.1 million.[32] Most of that money went toward the land purchase with the remainder for design and sponsorship and, with the exception of the pension trust, came from the stakeholders' general funds, an unusual decision.[33] As the project costs rose, so did the Janitors' Union stake until, at the time most of the union partners withdrew from the project, it reached between eleven and twelve million dollars.[34]

Given the project's scale and the increase in costs, additional lenders were essential. Estimated in mid-August 1959 at $21 million, including the towers' cost at $15 million, by February 1960 it had increased to $36 million and by July 1960 the towers were estimated at $18 million with another $10.6 million for the Janitors' Union's share of the project's commercial part.[35]

Although McFetridge, Swibel, and Goldberg had been successful in gaining mortgage insurance for most of the residential mortgage, the FHA could not insure loans on the project's nonresidential elements. To cover not only the residential towers' construction and mortgage costs but also the construction cost of the office complex, the theater, the bowling alley, the commercial platform, and so on—McFetridge and Swibel had to look to the private sector.[36] In November 1960, although the land had been purchased, this was still being negotiated.[37]

Following the conventional pattern, the project's funding was divided into two phases: short-term construction loans were followed by long-term mortgage loans. First, the complex's two parts required separate construction loans, one for the residential and one for the nonresidential element. The two construction loans were both provided by the Continental Illinois National Bank and Trust Company of Chicago (the Continental Illinois Bank), the seventh largest U.S. bank at the time. It loaned eighteen million dollars to build the residential towers and five million dollars to build the complex's commercial element.[38] The nonresidential construction loan formed another Chicago first: the largest commercial transaction in the city's real estate history and the second largest nationally after the Empire State Building's sale.[39]

The construction loans for the residential towers (eighteen million dollars) and nonresidential element (five million dollars) had to be replaced by long-term mortgages as soon as construction was completed. Although it took some time for it to commit to funding (it did so only following favorable reviews of Marina City in the Chicago press, aided by press releases from both BGA and Marks and Company), a consortium of East Coast banks, led by the Institutional Securities Corporation and Bay Ridge Savings Bank (the consortium), provided the residential mortgage.[40] The Continental Illinois Bank provided most of the nonresidential mortgage, not insured by the FHA. The Janitors' Union remained as the third stakeholder.[41] Other lenders followed in offering loans.[42] Swibel is reported to have orchestrated all of these deals.[43]

The Federal National Mortgage Association (Fannie Mae) had been on standby to purchase the residential mortgage had the consortium deal not materialized, but this would have cost the Janitors' Union close to an additional one million dollars. Given the project's private lenders' eventual financial collapse, today one might speculate how Marina City would have fared had Fannie Mae provided mortgage funding instead of the consortium.

With funding in place, borings for the foundations began, symbolically, on the day after Independence Day, July 5, 1960, and the groundbreaking ceremony took place on Thanksgiving Day 1960. The ceremony was a political and publicity spectacle. Mayor Daley, Archbishop Sheil, and other key

64. Marina City groundbreaking, Mayor Richard J. Daley, William McFetridge, and Charles Swibel, Chicago, IL, November 1960. Bertrand Goldberg Archive, Ryerson and Burnham Archives, The Art Institute of Chicago. © The Art Institute of Chicago.

Chicago leaders attended along with the Janitors' Union's national leadership; Daley, McFetridge, and Swibel basked in the limelight they created for their downtown vision. [Fig. 64]

In October 1960, to ease the Janitors' Union's huge financial commitment, another lender was brought to the project. General Electric (GE) agreed to loan the project two million dollars for the installation of electrical appliances throughout Marina City's buildings, at an interest of 5.75 percent, and Local 32B agreed to guarantee the General Electric loan. It formed another first: the largest loan that GE had ever made to a single project.[44]

Rentals

Despite an economic recession, in August 1961 the lease for the parking facility was signed. Promising low parking rates to tenants, it was said to be the largest of its kind in the nation.[45] McFetridge once again grasped this opportunity to laud his organization's efforts, reaffirming its role as guardian of below-market rate rentals for city workers. By September 1961, more than a year after construction began, the full financial package was completed. The Continental Illinois Bank, the consortium of financial institutions, and the various partners within the Janitors' Union remained the key stakeholders.[46] The Janitors' Union had bought into the commercial spaces as well as the residential towers; it held interest in the North Marina City Building Corporation, with one third of its share belonging to Janitors' Union Local 1, one sixth each by Janitors' Union Local 32B and the Janitors' Union Pension Trust (West Coast), and the final third held by the main Janitors' Union organization.[47]

The rentals in the building were calculated to generate profits for the stakeholders, to be affordable to tenants, and to meet the projections of the Chicago Central Area Committee. Estimated in 1959 to begin at $125 per month for studio apartments, $165 per month for a one-bedroom apartment, and $210 per month for a two-bedroom apartment, by the end of the following year these had changed: the efficiency apartment rentals ranged from $115 to $180 per month, the one-bedroom apartments from $155 to $230, and the two-bedroom apartments had increased to $295 to $350 per month. Electricity bills were foreseen at nine to thirteen dollars per month, but car-parking costs added a further $30 per month to rental costs.[48] The rentals were to appeal to Loop workers and by early 1962 there were 2,500 applicants for 896 apartments.[49] Echoing Goldberg, Swibel affirmed the benefits of Marina City's mixed-use program: "such rentals would be impossible if Marina City had not been designed to operate 24 hours with its complex of recreational and other facilities."[50] Goldberg, too, was involved in the process of finding tenants.[51]

By mid-1962 the office leases were also being signed. The office building was an experiment in low-cost rents, and its marketing language followed suit. Goldberg stated later, "The office building was technologically a very advanced building, but it was not a building that was super-elegant in finishes. We had no marble in it, we had limited stainless steel in it. It was a building that was at that time meant to open up a new area with attractive new rates for rents."[52] He invented a term, UNEX value, an acronym for unit-expense, for the office building marketing brochure and proposed that this would be lowered by features such as the proximity of housing, mixed-use amenities, and convenient parking: "UNEX (UNIT-EXPENSE) is the total expense of operating each unit of 1 square foot of office space. The square foot is the unit of measurement for the area of business space. UNEX (UNIT-EXPENSE) is the unit of measurement for the cost of business space."[53] The value of real estate was thus to be driven not only by construction cost but also by surrounding amenities—highlighting the hidden additional market value in an urban mixed-use development. No dollar sum, however, was included in the brochure to quantify such amenities.

In August 1962 WCFL, the radio station of the Chicago Federation of Labor, signed a lease for the top floor of the office building and moved into the building in late 1964. Also in 1962 the National Design Center signed a lease for thirty-five-thousand square feet of the office building—a significant expansion over its former New York facilities.[54] Later, the Sperry Rand Corporation, a computer hardware company, moved into the office building, adding another progressive tenant to the complex. In 1964 the newly founded Marina City Bank negotiated a lease in the office building and by February 1965 was reported by the Illinois Banker magazine to have twelve million dollars in deposits.[55] In the same article the Continental Illinois Bank was also noted for its high earnings. Also in 1964 the office building gained additional commercial tenants, signing a lease with the State Highway Department and a lease for the bowling alley space.[56] The television station WFLD also became a tenant in the office building but only began broadcasting when the theater building was finally finished in January 1966. BGA also moved into the office building upon its completion. Swibel's connections had helped attract key tenants but the Janitors' Union's vast national network of influence and Goldberg's design circles had also been useful.

In 1964 the Hilton Hotels Corporation began to operate the dining room and cocktail lounge within the commercial platform. By 1967 leases had been issued to a number of stores, among them Marina City Drugs and Liquors, Chalmers Food supermarket, a Fannie May chocolate and candy counter, a Viennese-style snack shop, a florist, a travel agency, a second cocktail lounge, a dry cleaning store, a beauty shop, and an American Health Studio spa. The commercial tenancies employed 1,500 workers.[57] Although the offices were not yet fully rented, the Marina City complex was bustling with life; over two-and-a-half thousand people were now living or working there.

The residential towers had also more or less met their rental goals. By late 1963, 81 percent of the apartments were let.[58] In 1967 the tenants were composed of one-third single men, one-third single women, and one-third married couples; they were teachers, attorneys, judges, secretaries, school principals, engineers, interior decorators, models, TV people, and so on. The average tenant's income was between twelve and thirteen thousand dollars per year (the national mean that year was $8,801); although these were not low or average incomes, the results were skewed by some very high-income tenants attracted to the location and the complex's image.[59] Rents had increased to between $165 and $200 per month for one-bedroom apartments on lower floors—on the top twenty floors these now cost up to $230 per month.[60]

The tenancy of the theater building, however, proved hard to tackle. It had to be pre-let before BGA could complete the theater design, perhaps explaining why the office had the time to explore more than one structural and planning solution. Goldberg later commented:

> The fact that the theater building had so much difficulty in becoming a reality also was an unpleasant surprise. Here we are, looking for a suitable house for the Goodman Theatre, and a theater building exists at Marina City that will seat 1,400 or 1,500 people. You can have two more theaters—a rehearsal theater and a small theater for more intimate productions—all in one building, and it's empty.[61]

Only with WFLD's arrival was the theater's interior planning completed. The project began to generate revenue for the city. In 1961 taxation income was projected to be more than half a million dollars annually.[62] Daley's downtown revitalization initiative benefited not only from Marina City's taxes but also from the project's impact on other downtown development. John Waner declared that his office was processing another twenty million dollars in downtown residential projects modeled on Marina City.[63] Goldberg's vision of integrated inner-city living was taking root.

In March 1961, a month after the boosterist statement by Waner, the *Chicago Sun-Times* reported that twenty-six major buildings had been built or started in the past three years alone. The Chicago Central Area Committee commented that the nearly $250 million spent on new buildings during this time almost equaled the cost of rebuilding after the Great Chicago Fire and up to January 1, 1890.[64] By November 1961, it was claimed that since the start of Marina City, five hundred million dollars of other downtown projects had been announced and, by February 1963, with the end of the recession, the value of the Marina City land was reputed to also have increased from twenty to thirty dollars per square foot.[65]

Union Wars

Despite its success as an urban catalyst, Marina City had its detractors from the beginning. Already at the time of the groundbreaking the United States was heading into a recession and by early 1961 was in major economic slowdown. The recession brought the first criticisms. Negative articles began to appear, such as "The Union and Marina City," published in 1961 in an Iowa construction journal and sent to the Janitors' Union's headquarters. The author lamented, "Management…is deeply concerned by the union's use of the welfare fund to finance Marina City. The union accumulated this fund from the monthly contributions of property owners—and now uses the fund to directly compete with and possibly destroy the property owners," and added, "How wise an investment for the union was Marina City? If our economy should falter...it could sacrifice its interest, and millions of dollars already invested...at a time when the money was most desperately needed for the workers' welfare."[66] Attached to this anonymous mailing was an article from the *Chicago Daily Tribune* dated February 8, 1961, that also blamed the government for exempting the unions from antitrust provisions governing monopolistic practice.

The most powerful detractor, however, was David Sullivan, the Janitors' Union's president. Internal conflict, with Marina City at its center, had erupted already in early 1960. Following Sullivan's appointment to the presidency, McFetridge was said to be disappointed with his protégé, and fought to remove Sullivan as president. When he failed he turned to keeping control of Marina City in Chicago hands rather than the Janitors' Union's executive board.[67]

By 1961 internal memos began warning various stakeholders that Swibel's efforts to refinance the project would require additional Janitors' Union funds and that McFetridge was rumored to be trying to get out of the project. The question of the project's control reemerged in 1962, reviving McFetridge's earlier promise to union stakeholders to act as directors of the two Marina City corporations, and never again died down. The executive board again demanded full access to Marina City decision-making.[68] McFetridge refused and through 1962 and 1963 neither Sullivan nor the board were able to pressure him to change the arrangement.[69] Heated meetings and phone calls involved the board, McFetridge, Swibel, and Sidney Korshak, McFetridge's personal counsel (deeply compromised through his role as the union's attorney in its mob-friendly Scalise days) and centered on control and funding, without resolution.

Despite the revival in the economy, by 1963 the leadership of the Janitors' Union, steered doggedly by Jay Raskin, treasurer of the Pension Trust (West Coast), insisted that Marina City's return on investment would be less than 3 percent and that the project was seven or eight million dollars short of funds needed for completion.[70] This was much less than the 7 percent return on its capital investment originally anticipated by the Janitors' Union, which also expected full equity once the mortgages were paid off.[71] Moreover, the organization was reported to be "contingently liable" for loans from the Continental Illinois Bank and feared that Local 1 would not be able to pay notes coming due in 1964.[72] Sullivan asked the union's auditors to review the project and pushed for the sale of the union's interests.[73] The battle came to a head at the Janitors' Union's meeting in Los Angeles in May 1964 with the union's decision to "get out" of Marina City.[74] By July 1964 Sullivan was claiming that Marina City rentals were too expensive for union workers and therefore did not support the union's mission.

Sullivan also attacked the complex's design and location, claiming that these had led to increased costs: "the unusual architecture plus underground construction problems resulting from its riverfront location have caused the project to cost more and take longer to complete than anticipated."[75] Other national civic leaders also criticized the project. D. W. Martin of the United Housing Foundation had written to the Janitors' Union stating, "from the rent schedule, only the wealthy can afford to enjoy it. I hope the day is not far off when your union will sponsor a cooperative within the means of your members and other wage earners."[76]

The Janitors' Union and Local 32B withdrew their support. Their financial interests, with the exception of McFetridge's still loyal Local 1, were bought out by Swibel's Marina City Management Corporation.[77] According to Swibel, the corporation now owned a two-thirds stake in the residential complex, with Local 1 holding most of the other third—an enormous amount as by then, the project's cost was said to be in excess of thirty-eight million dollars.[78] General Electric continued to hold its share of just under two million dollars. Nevertheless, the ever-loyal *Chicago Sun-Times* reported that McFetridge, "rebuffed in other efforts at the Los Angeles convention of the Building Service Employees International Union, which he once headed, won a major victory: He will retain control of Marina City Towers."[79] John F. Mannion, Continental Illinois Bank's senior vice-president added that "with this transaction, all Chicagoans can now take pride in Marina City as an all-Chicago project."[80]

Marina City Management

Swibel's star was also waning. Although he now held a huge stake in the Marina City complex—and his brother Maurice Swibel ran the Marina City Management Corporation, which was in charge of the rentals—his role in Marks and Company, and also at the Chicago Housing Authority, had become increasingly fraught.[81] In late 1963 the *Chicago Courier* reported that already in 1953 Marks and Company had been investigated by the *Chicago Daily News* as "one of the top 20 firms engaged in slum operations, ownership or financing" and accused Swibel's firm of racism.[82] By April 1966 the City of Chicago was suing Swibel for illegal conversion and poor maintenance of Marks and Company buildings. Swibel resigned as president of Marks and Company but the new vice-president filed a lawsuit against him citing misappropriation of more than two million dollars from trusts administered by the company.[83] Although the lawsuit never came to court and Swibel continued at the CHA, this was not good publicity for the Janitors' Union given its history of corruption under Scalise.[84]

In 1967 the North Marina City Building Corporation declared it was unable to meet the repayments of the commercial mortgage to the Continental Illinois Bank, reported at sixteen million dollars.[85] The Continental Illinois Bank took over NMCBC's interests and also those of Local 1, the once loyal base of the now ailing McFetridge.[86] In a full circle, the original agent for the land purchase, L. J. Sheridan, was hired by the bank to manage the complex, with Swibel remaining as managing agent.[87] The Janitors' Union was now finally fully out of the project. McFetridge would die two years later.

A thirty-year period of financial neglect of the complex began. In 1977 the residential towers were converted to condominiums, which though profitable for the owners, further escalated costs for tenants. Swibel reportedly made more than six million dollars by buying apartments at insider prices and flipping them.[88] The Continental Illinois Bank failed in 1984 as part of the Penn Square Bank N.A. of Oklahoma collapse. At the time, it was the largest bank to be bailed out by the Federal Deposit Insurance Corporation (FDIC) and the Federal Reserve. In 1983 Marina City Associates, a Texas Real Estate Investment Trust, purchased the commercial elements of Marina City. The Continental Savings Association of Houston provided the mortgage to Marina City Associates. It filed for foreclosure in 1987 and was taken over by the Federal Savings and Loan Insurance Corporation; soon afterwards Marina City Associates declared bankruptcy.[89] Thus, although the apartments continued to attract rentals, the bankruptcy of the commercial spaces dragged down the real estate appeal of the entire complex.

In the late 1990s, during the last decade of Goldberg's life, the complex experienced a revival of fortune. The theater was redeveloped as a House of Blues performance venue and the office building as a House of Blues hotel. Renovation of the complex's retail and commercial parts followed. The disused ice rink was filled in and became a steak house. Some of these changes were architecturally problematic; nevertheless the involvement of the Goldberg office—reportedly due to pressure exerted on the developers by the city—preserved threatened elements of the complex such as the theater, sacrificing only those which could be easily restored to their original form later. Though in the 1970s and 1980s he had not been able to stem the complex's decline, before his death in 1997 Goldberg thus once again played a significant role in Marina City's future.

Profit and Loss

The financial tale of Marina City is a cautionary one. Although the "city within a city" was based on innovative urban and financial strategies, for a significant period it became a victim of its own financial and urban success and then of its stakeholders' greed. Economic change also played a role. Inevitably, the project's increased value—a measure of its success—resulted in property tax increases that were passed on to the tenants.[90] The refinancing of the original real estate deals, and in particular the apartments' transformation into condominiums, raised property values and taxes beyond middle-income pockets. The uninsured commercial loan left a significant part of Marina City fully exposed to the market's ups and downs. Thus in 1967, when the Continental Illinois Bank bought out the Janitors' Union's commercial interests, it was left with all the financial risk for the complex's nonresidential component.[91] The insured towers remained a safer investment. And profit—rather than the project's social vision—formed a greater motivating force for the Janitors' Union, Swibel, the Continental Illinois Bank, and the consortium.[92] Finally, the global economic crises of the 1970s and 1980s, of which the collapse of the project's main lenders were important vignettes, played a powerful role in Marina City's long, if nevertheless impermanent, neglect.

These factors, beyond the influence of union leaders, realtors, architects, or politicians, helped erode the Marina City complex's original social mandate. Projects of its financial scale and ambition inevitably carried huge financial risks and during the economic downturns of the 1970s, 1980s, and 1990s, the entire Chicago downtown experienced deep disinvestment. Only recently with new real estate investment have Marina City's finances stabilized, but this occured at a cost both to the original proposal's architecture and urban vision.

Yet, in the long-term, Marina City proved extremely resilient both as a piece of property and a desirable Chicago location to "work and play." It has retained its prominent presence in the Chicago skyline, in tourist itineraries, and within popular memory, and it once again receives positive attention from the local press and national architectural journals. Most importantly, it remains a powerful example of a public-private partnership that created an important model for social mobility, urban revitalization, fiscal creativity, and architectural and engineering innovation.

chapter five

the image

PETER CARUSO ON THE JET SET, JUST BACK FROM EUROPE,
REPORTS CHICAGO'S IMAGE, AT LONG LAST, IS CHANGING.
IN MANY PLACES HE WAS GREETED, AS A CHICAGOAN, WITH
THE USUAL RAT-A-TAT OF A MACHINE GUN. BUT IN A GROWING
NUMBER OF SITUATIONS CARUSO REPORTS, THE REACTION
WAS "CHICAGO? AH, MARINA CITY TOWERS."

—*CHICAGO SUN-TIMES*, 1966

The ebb and flow of Marina City's real estate value was intimately connected to its media presence, a central concern of the project partners from the very beginning. Always an investment in urban renewal, it also stood as a symbol of a city, its architecture and culture. Officials, realtors, and banks first forged its value, but writers, critics, and journalists also created Marina City. It was not only a real estate commodity but also an icon appearing frequently in architecture magazines, exhibitions, and films. Marina City's real estate value and architectural images intertwined in a symbiotic relationship, providing perhaps the most significant role for its architect. Bertrand Goldberg communicated Marina City's image using a variety of representational strategies for different audiences—the FHA, the Janitors' Union, the Chicago public, and the international architectural community. From the beginning the complex was advertised as an embodiment of many exciting architectural firsts:

> First circular apartment towers in history, first helical parking ramps for apartments, first theatre of its type, first use of window frames as structural members, on and on. In the international world of architecture, Chicago's first downtown housing project is sure to create a considerable stir.[1]

Other firsts in the marketing of "bigness" included the tallest apartment structure in the world, the only all-electric city, the largest federal mortgage insurance, the biggest land sale, and so on. Such bold advertising was augmented by renderings of the complex in a variety of media, which relied on an intricate play of marketing and high design.

←
**65. "Marina City Christmas Lights,"
Marina City (1959–1967), Chicago, IL,
1971.** Charles Kirman [photographer]. Tripod mounted camera rotated 360 degrees during a 15 second time exposure with additional images added by multiple exposure. By permission of Charles Kirman. Bertrand Goldberg Archive, Ryerson and Burnham Archives, The Art Institute of Chicago. © The Art Institute of Chicago.

An unprecedented media blitz accompanied Marina City's launch. Goldberg's office developed many news releases, as well as two- and three-dimensional images of Marina City, which were produced for different purposes. Architectural drawings and models were used for statutory approvals; full-scale models and printed brochures were meant for lay audiences; and texts and photographs in architectural, planning, and construction journals targeted construction industry professionals. These strategies suggest that Goldberg understood the built environment's value as being produced and reproduced through visual media as much as through its physical form.[2] Traveling around the world with unprecedented speed, Marina City's image played an important role in its reception, framing the historical understanding of the complex. These marketing strategies, coupled with the press' favorable coverage of Marina City during its planning, were so successful that it led the consortium to approve the mortgage for Marina City despite initially declining it.[3]

Goldberg's targeted use of drawings, photographs, and installations paralleled similar efforts by contemporary U.S. and European architects who visualized homes of the future through "good design" using the printed image and film. The Case Study Houses of California designed by U.S. architects—including Ray and Charles Eames, Richard Neutra, Craig Ellwood, Eero Saarinen, and Pierre Koenig—formed one set of built examples. Sponsored by *Arts and Architecture* magazine, the Case Study Houses were heavily published in the magazine and in subsequent books; John Entenza, the editor, was a close friend of the Goldberg family and Bertrand Goldberg, would have been well aware of the importance of publication in the reputation of the Case Study Houses. A European, if unbuilt counterpart, This is Tomorrow, a 1956 exhibition and catalog organized by Theo Crosby, editor of *Architectural Design* magazine, included the work of architects working in the United Kingdom—such as Alison and Peter Smithson, James Stirling, Ernö Goldfinger, Colin St John Wilson, and Frank Newby. Both examples drew heavily on associated publications for their impact and both targeted consumers: the Case Study Houses were designed to be replicable, and This is Tomorrow integrated high and popular culture, spearheading British pop art's emergence. The "imaging" of Marina City thus occurred at a time when architects were starting to market their work directly to consumers and when architectural photography's popularity was increasing in magazines and exhibitions, a cultural condition with which Goldberg was familiar.

The imaging of Marina City also sprang from a more personal trajectory. Goldberg's sensitivity to theater and publicity owed something to the Bauhaus tradition of theater and student festivals, as well as to its teaching and practice of graphic design and advertising. This early history of publicity and performance fed nearly twenty years of marketing efforts in the Goldberg office before Marina City; in addition Goldberg loved to write about his work and that of others and had produced several "books."[4] It is therefore not surprising that he played a key role in marketing Marina City, orchestrating photographs, installations, and public events, and writing marketing text.

Models, Drawings, and Collages

The visualization of Marina City began with conventional drawings, collages, and models. The Goldberg office used models early to study Marina City's shape. A 1959 study model showed three circular towers similar to Goldberg's Astor Tower—the building's main volume raised above the ground, the concrete

66. **Lucite model, Marina City (1959–1967), Bertrand Goldberg Associates, Chicago, IL.** Hedrich-Blessing [photographer]. HB-23215-C, Bertrand Goldberg Archive, Ryerson and Burnham Archives, The Art Institute of Chicago. Digital File # 200203.081229-278. Courtesy of The Art Institute of Chicago. © The Chicago History Museum

67. **Marina City model at the Continental Illinois Bank, Chicago, IL, August 1961.** Bertrand Goldberg Archive, Ryerson and Burnham Archives, The Art Institute of Chicago. Digital File #200203.081229-270 © The Art Institute of Chicago.

core visible and framed by columns, and a shorter office building located on a separate raised platform.[5] A later study model showed Marina City in Lucite, a Plexiglas-like medium, known to Goldberg via Lillian Florsheim's artwork, which lent itself more easily to curved organic forms. [Fig. 66] Later, the office produced a large and very detailed scale model of the Marina City complex located for years in the Marina City lobby. Showing people, cars, and trees, and used for marketing, it was heavily reproduced in the media.

This model was also documented through many photographs by Hedrich-Blessing. That firm's night and day shots anticipated the project's luminous nighttime presence and sharply shadowed daytime form. It was often used in collages and exhibitions presenting Marina City to the Chicago public and the Janitors' Union. In 1961 the model was displayed to Chicagoans at an exhibition at the Continental Illinois Bank Building, with labels identifying program elements while a background panel described the complex's main amenities.[6] [Fig. 67] The base included light switches for illuminating different locations: the shops, parking, the plaza, the skating rink, restaurant, and so on. The panel included a list of the project partners, an estimated construction time of seventeen months, images of the Marina City site with its rising concrete floors, and language advertising the apartments as "rooms with a view." These early images communicated a sense of excitement about Marina City's form and structural innovation. They also show the importance of viewing and vision in the branding of Marina City.

Goldberg also used drawings to achieve different goals with different publics. The first drawings of the project were diagrams on paper, presenting basic formal and organizational concepts to the Janitors' Union. The first Marina City scheme, the Labor Center, is a perfect example. Drawings of the "square scheme," on the other hand, were created only to gain FHA approval. A third and different set of drawings was used to gain zoning approval.

In addition to conventional orthogonal drawings, BGA used perspective renderings to visualize Marina City. These echoed the period's style, using tone to create strong contrasts. One such rendering, pairing modern with traditional form, showed Marina City soaring above the nearby Wrigley Building (1924) and Chicago Tribune Tower (1925). [Fig. 68] Its more intimate companion piece showed the public space between buildings and people strolling around the skating rink with Marina City Theater's glazed interior in the background. [Fig. 69] The plaza open space contained planters and trees, with sculptures as well as an ethereal painting in the foreground. The carefully positioned vanishing points of the plaza and the public art heightened the artworks' presence, connecting the buildings' structural expressionism with the sculpture's formal expressionism. Establishing a continuum of art, architecture, and urbanism, the rendering's content and style clearly intended to appeal to a visually literate and progressive audience.

Another group of images included an expressionist drawing, with broad brushstrokes emphasizing the Marina City Theater interior's aerodynamic quality. [Fig. 70] The medium's "wetness" created a subjective representation with details only visible in the foreground, while the background recedes into a series of curved perspectival lines. The backlit curved screen and the first few rows of chairs with built-in lights were clearly visible, as were the inflatable domes forming the acoustic ceiling, treated in an expressive, even romantic fashion. Given that this design was never realized, we wonder for whom the drawing was intended.

68. River view rendering, Marina City (1959–1967), Bertrand Goldberg Associates, Chicago, IL. Bertrand Goldberg Archive, Ryerson and Burnham Archives, The Art Institute of Chicago. © The Art Institute of Chicago.

69. Plaza level rendering, Marina City (1959–1967), Bertrand Goldberg Associates, Chicago, IL. Bertrand Goldberg Archive, Ryerson and Burnham Archives, The Art Institute of Chicago. Digital File #200203.081229-268 © The Art Institute of Chicago.

70. Theater, interior rendering,
Marina City (1959–1967), Bertrand
Goldberg Associates, Chicago, IL.
Photograph. Bertrand Goldberg Archive, Ryerson
and Burnham Archives, The Art Institute of Chicago.
© The Art Institute of Chicago.

71. Marina and Phillips Pier 66, Marina
City (1959–1967), Bertrand Goldberg
Associates, Chicago, IL. R. A. Johnson
[photographer]. Bertrand Goldberg Archive, Ryerson and
Burnham Archives, The Art Institute of Chicago. Digital File
#200203.081229-243 © The Art Institute of Chicago.

ROOF LEVEL & TOWERS

— 40 STORY APARTMENT BLDG.
— 10 STORY OFFICE BLDG
— 40 STORY APARTMENT BLDG
— ROOF TERRACE & GARDENS

MARINA CITY
CHICAGO, ILLINOIS

BERTRAND GOLDBERG ASSOCIATES — — —ARCHITECTS & ENGINEERS

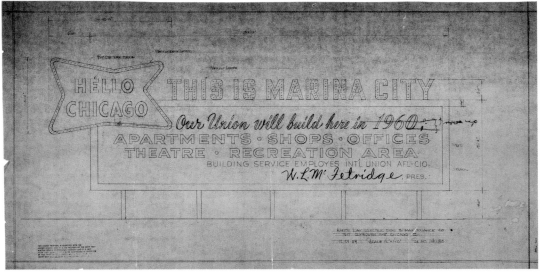

72. Square towers design variation, Marina City (1959–1967), Bertrand Goldberg Associates, Chicago, IL, February 1960. Bertrand Goldberg Archive, Ryerson and Burnham Archives, The Art Institute of Chicago. © The Art Institute of Chicago.

73. "Hello Chicago, This is Marina City," White Way Electric Sign and Maintenance Co., 1959. By permission of White Way Electric Sign and Maintenance Co. Bertrand Goldberg Archive, Architecture and Design Department, Art Institute of Chicago.

A black-and-white rendering focuses on the marina and commercial platform. [Fig. 71] Showing people on the walkway above the marina and behind the commercial platform's floor-to-ceiling glass facade, this drawing, with its two-point-perspective technical precision, demonstrates the office's capacity for realistic representation. It addressed a slightly different audience, the workmanlike drawing and the small scale of the motor boat representing a working man's boating paradise.

In addition to drawings for public consumption, BGA also produced drawn design explorations to support decision-making. Marina City's relatively complex geometry required projective drawings to determine form, materiality, and structure. For example, the theater with its complex curvature posed a particular challenge.

BGA also used collage to visualize Marina City. This format eventually evolved into elaborate depictions of models within urban skylines. An early example shows the project as an axonometric with square towers inserted within an aerial photograph of the site—a more realistic depiction for both the FHA and the public. [Fig. 72] It appeared in several publications, including the outboard industry's trade publication. The collage was a "tamed" version of Marina City, which was bold enough as a program, let alone as an unusual shape. Goldberg said, "My early drawings on that building are for two rectangular towers. I didn't dare show anybody the circular towers."[7] Thus this image of square towers was used early on to rally the public and the FHA behind the idea of Marina City.

Construction drawings too went beyond the regular drawing set of the period to exquisitely detail the formal and technical ambitions of the complex. The office developed numerous details in both the towers and the office building. Exploratory construction drawings also investigated a myriad of other issues including mullions, boat-moving, and "Dinopacker"—the mechanized trash disposal mentioned in "The Structure" chapter.

Even before the Marina City site was fully cleared for construction, a large billboard was erected there facing the river, stating "Hello Chicago, This is Marina City." [Fig. 73] Designed to appeal to the general public, the text was not in modernism's sans serif typeface but instead in the streamlined Moderne typeface typical of drive-ins. Given its visibility from the Loop, the billboard piqued Chicagoans' interest and allowed the project triumvirate—Goldberg, McFetridge, and Swibel—a more public presence.

Groundbreaking Ceremony and Brochure

The Marina City marketing campaign also involved the careful orchestration of public events. In the groundbreaking ceremony, held on Thanksgiving Day, November 22, 1960, multiple promotional tools—photographs, plaques, special publications, and press coverage—coalesced. The guests, in formal dress, gathered under a large marquee on the site to witness the pouring of the first batch of concrete. [Fig. 74] As the groundbreaking program testified, the ceremony included some of the most prominent Chicago figures.[8]

McFetridge, as the Marina City Building Corporation's president and the Janitors' Union's former president, provided opening and closing remarks. *Benedictio ad omnia* (Blessing for all things) was given by Archbishop Sheil. "Greetings to Marina City" were presented by David Sullivan, newly elected Janitors' Union president. Julian H. Zimmerman of the FHA, Daniel "Dan" Ryan, president of the Cook County Board of Commissioners, and John Waner,

74. Marina City groundbreaking ceremony, from left to right: Thomas Young, David Sullivan, unknown, Richard J. Daley, William L. McFetridge, Bernard Sheil, Charles Swibel, and Bertrand Goldberg; Chicago, IL, November 22, 1960. Bertrand Goldberg Archive, Ryerson and Burnham Archives, The Art Institute of Chicago. Digital File #200203.081229-340 © The Art Institute of Chicago.

75. Marina City groundbreaking ceremony, Chicago civic leaders dressed as "Sons of (John) Kinzie" with William McFetridge, wearing glasses, center, Chicago, IL, November 22, 1960. Bertrand Goldberg Archive, Ryerson and Burnham Archives, The Art Institute of Chicago. © The Art Institute of Chicago.

76. Marina City groundbreaking ceremony, William McFetridge on the phone to President-elect John F. Kennedy, November 22, 1960. Bertrand Goldberg Archive, Ryerson and Burnham Archives, The Art Institute of Chicago. Digital File #200203.081229-341 © The Art Institute of Chicago.

director of the Chicago FHA, all attended. Listed as Sons of Kinzie, other notable Chicago entrepreneurs and leaders presented their talks under the umbrella
of Sullivan's "Greetings to Marina City."[9] [**Fig. 75**]

Hedrich-Blessing documented the groundbreaking ceremony in many
photographs. A particularly interesting image showed McFetridge in a historic
moment on the telephone to President-elect John F. Kennedy—an aspect of
the ceremony representing the project's importance within the national political environment. [**Fig. 76**] The Janitors' Union, BGA, and the Case Foundation
Company orchestrated the ceremony—with its extensive guest list, photographic
documentation, and brochure—to form the Chicago public relations event of the
year.

Attendees at the groundbreaking ceremony were proudly shown a brochure titled *Marina City: A New Dimension in Urban Living.* [**Fig. 77**] This was
a large, rectangular, and beautifully designed publication. Embodying civic
pride and political ambition, it was intended for an audience within and beyond
Chicago. Its cover comprised a vellum reprint of an 1810 drawing of Fort
Dearborn, which once occupied the site, overlaid on a nighttime-view photograph of the Marina City model. The years 1810 and 1960 were inscribed in
large numerals on vellum and paper respectively, emphasizing the Marina City
development's historical importance in the city's history (see Fig. 74).

The brochure opened with a short introductory text by McFetridge.[10] It
included the showroom portrait of McFetridge gazing dreamily at the Chicago
skyline (see Fig. 80). McFetridge used the brochure to remind the Janitors'
Union's 270,000 members that Marina City was ethical and in their best financial interest. By helping rebuild the declining city core, the complex would create jobs and new lives for janitors. He wanted to share that message with his
political and civic peers as well as the public:

> Marina City is the translation of a daring plan into an exciting reality. Such
> ideas are not rare; such realities are. As the tangible realization of a truly mod-
> ern idea, Marina City has become the center of world interest in urban plan-
> ning on its most promising scale. What is accomplished in—and by—Marina
> City will be noted and responded to in many places. Marina City takes this
> opportunity to invite others who may be inclined to translate ideas into real-
> ities—to become part of this exciting, rewarding focal point of urban living.[11]

McFetridge's heroic tone was to rally Chicagoans to his vision—and perhaps to address the Janitors' Union's emerging doubts. He also reminded his
audiences of the importance of international media attention to the project—
showing his understanding of the power of publicity and media opinion in the
project's status and realization.

The groundbreaking ceremony was immortalized a year later in a celestial
map, presented to the Marina City team on Thanksgiving Day, 1961, by a politi-
cally astute Chicago Planetarium Society.[12] [**Fig. 78**] The map documented the
star positions on the date of the groundbreaking ceremony. Its short caption in
five languages—English, Latin, Greek, Hebrew, and Chinese—was inscribed on
a copper scroll, and it was embedded in the East Tower's core to be preserved
for future archaeologists.[13] All attendees were given a paper version of the copper map, in a tube, handed out like scrolls. Idealistic and romantic, the *Celestial
Map* and its celebration added yet another occasion to the many events keeping
public attention focused on Marina City's progress.

↗
**77. Marina City Groundbreaking,
brochure (vellum removed), 1960.**
Bertrand Goldberg Archive, Ryerson and Burnham
Archives, The Art Institute of Chicago. © The Art
Institute of Chicago.

→
**78. Celestial Map, showing the
positions of stars on November 22, 1960,
the day of Marina City's groundbreaking
ceremony, Chicago Planetarium Society,
1961.** Photograph. By permission of the Adler
Planetarium. Bertrand Goldberg Archive, Ryerson and
Burnham Archives, The Art Institute of Chicago.
© The Art Institute of Chicago.

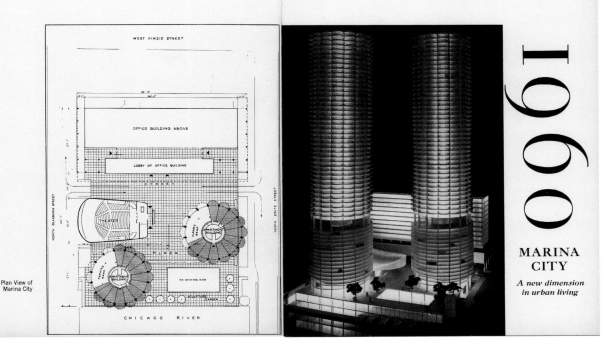

Plan View of
Marina City

1960

MARINA CITY

*A new dimension
in urban living*

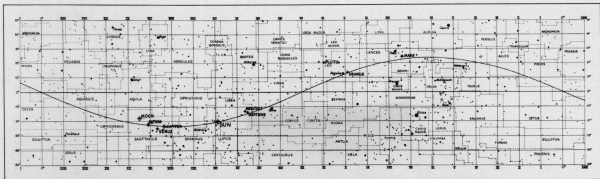

THIS BUILDING BEGAN ON THE 22nd DAY OF NOVEMBER 1960 A.D. ACCORDING TO THE GREGORIAN CALENDAR.

THE PLANETS IN THE HEAVENS WERE AS SHOWN ON THIS CELESTIAL MAP. THE UNIVERSAL LANGUAGE OF ASTRONOMY WILL PERMIT MEN FOREVER TO UNDERSTAND AND KNOW THIS DATE.

MARINA CITY AND ITS TOWERS WERE THE DREAM OF WILLIAM L. McFETRIDGE, THE PLANNING OF CHARLES R. SWIBEL, AND THE ARCHITECTURE OF BERTRAND GOLDBERG.

INCEPTVM EST AEDIFICARI A. D. X KAL. DEC. ANNO SALVTIS MCMLX.

ID TEMPORIS ERRANTES STELLAE VT IN TABVLA FEREBANTVR. HOMINVM LINGVAE VARIAE VARIE MVTANTVR SED STELLARVM LOQVELA IN AETERNVM FIXA.

HANC INSVLAM TVRRIGERAM VRBEM IN RIPA NVNCVPATAM EXCOGITAVIT GVLIELMVS DE PATRICIIS FACIENDVM CVRAVIT CAROLVS SWIBELIVS FECIT BERNARDVS DE MONTE AVREO.

ΗΡΞΑΝΤΟ ΟΙΚΟΔΟΜΕΙΝ ΤΟΥΤΟ ΤΗΣ ΧΙΛΙΑ ΟΛΥΜΠΙΑΔΟΣ ΕΤΕΙ Δ ΜΑΙΜΑΚΤΗΡΙΩΝΟΣ ΔΕΥΤΕΡΑΙ ΦΘΙΝΟΝΤΟΣ

ΕΙΧΟΝ ΔΕ ΤΟΤΕ ΠΡΟΣ ΑΛΛΗΛΟΥΣ ΟΙ ΠΛΑΝΗΤΑΙ ΩΣ ΕΝ ΤΗΙ ΠΙΝΑΚΙ ΔΕΔΗΛΩΤΑΙ · ΑΝΘΡΩΠΩΝ ΜΕΝ ΓΑΡ ΔΙΑΛΕΚΤΟΙ ΠΟΛΛΑΙ · ΤΩΝ ΔΕ ΟΥΡΑΝΙΩΝ ΜΙΑ ΦΩΝΗ ΚΑΙ Η ΑΥΤΗ ΗΛΣΙΝ

ΑΥΤΗ Η ΔΙΠΥΡΓΟΣ ΣΥΝΟΙΚΙΑ ΕΠΙΠΟΤΑΜΙΣ ΚΑΛΟΥΜΕΝΗ ΟΙΚΟΔΟΜΗΘΗ ΓΝΩΜΗΙ ΜΕΝ ΓΥΛΙΕΛΜΟΥ ΕΠΙΜΕΛΕΙΑΙ ΔΕ ΚΑΡΟΛΟΥ ΤΕΧΝΗΙ ΔΕ ΒΕΡΝΑΡΔΟΥ

הקמתו של הבנין הזהלה ביום ה-22 לחודש נובמבר, שנת 1960 לפי הלוח הגריגוריאני. מערכת הכוכבים היתה כמתואר כמפת - שמים זו; שפת האסטרונומיה האוניברסלית תאפשר להבין ולהכיר תאריך זה לעולם.

בנין ״מרינה סיטי״ ומגדליו שהיו חלום של וילאם ל. מקפטרידג׳, תכננו ע״י צ׳רלס ר. סוויבל לפי ארכיטקטורה של ברטרנד גולדברג.

大廈於西曆一九六零年十一月二十二日開始鳩工興建．天體圖上即表明是日行星所處之位置，以象徵團結如之天文學語言使人類永久和悉此一日期．

麥林邪市大廈繫其希望培德偉威廉．麥克菲特瑞基之理遇；查理．斯威伯爾之設計，又栢特監哥爾特伯格之建築．

79. Balcony with panorama, full-scale
Marina City showroom apartment
at 316 West Randolph Street, Bertrand
Goldberg Associates, Chicago, IL, 1962.
Hedrich-Blessing [photographer]. HB-23215-B7,
Chicago History Museum.

80. William McFetridge leaning against
balcony railing, Marina City showroom
apartment at 316 West Randolph Street,
Bertrand Goldberg Associates, Chicago,
IL, 1962. Hedrich-Blessing [photographer].
HB-23215-A7, Chicago History Museum.

81. Bertrand Goldberg (left) and Ira Bach, Chicago Planning Commissioner, Marina City showroom apartment at 316 West Randolph Street, Bertrand Goldberg Associates, Chicago, IL, 1962. Mart Studios Inc., [photograph] Bertrand Goldberg Archive, Ryerson and Burnham Archives, The Art Institute of Chicago. © The Art Institute of Chicago.

Showrooms: Apartments and Offices

One of the most interesting strategies involved in imaging Marina City was building full-scale replicas of apartments for marketing. Proposed by Goldberg based on his experience with Unicel, they were funded by the Janitors' Union at a cost of fifty-thousand dollars—a significant sum—and opened to the public in January 1962 at 316 West Randolph Street, the Janitors' Union's headquarters.[14] Comprising two-and-a-half fully constructed petals of Marina City, the showroom featured decorated, furnished, and lit efficiency and one-bedroom apartments with semicircular balconies facing a photographic panorama of the city beyond. [Fig. 79] Taken from a helicopter flying at the level of the imaginary Marina City towers' fortieth floor, the seventy-feet wide aerial view was mounted on a curved wall, representing the romance of living in the tallest residential building in the world.

The showrooms helped explain the project not only to potential funders and renters, but it also formed a showcase for Goldberg, McFetridge, and Swibel. McFetridge's most imposing Marina City publicity photo, taken by Hedrich-Blessing, positioned him on the balcony of his "dream" apartment. [Fig. 80] Another image documented Ira Bach and Goldberg in front of the panorama, with Bach pointing into the distance. [Fig. 81]

Hedrich-Blessing photographs of the showroom apartments contrasted the drama of outdoor spaces with the comfort of interiors. In the living room, open curtains revealed a view of the balcony and Chicago skyline. The balcony dining table, framed by small circular planters showed this outdoor space as another living room—an extension of the interior into an urban room in the sky. Hedrich-Blessing paired daylight and nighttime images of the same space. [Figs. 82 and 83] The night view combined the controlled light of domestic lamps with a spotlit view of the modern metropolis beyond while the daylight image led the eye to a brightly lit balcony and panorama. While the day view had a breakfast table laid out on the balcony, the night image showed a neatly laid dinner table in the dining area inside the unit. Apart from fruit, a candlestick, and table settings, decoration was minimal, with no people in either image. Nevertheless the setting's theatricality was unquestionable; although there were no actual

82. Living room with daylight simulation, Marina City showroom apartment at 316 West Randolph Street, Bertrand Goldberg Associates, Chicago, IL, 1962. Hedrich-Blessing [photographer], 1962. HB-23215-Q, Chicago History Museum.

←

82. Living room with daylight simulation, Marina City showroom apartment at 316 West Randolph Street, Bertrand Goldberg Associates, Chicago, IL, 1962. Hedrich-Blessing [photographer], 1962. HB-23215-Q, Chicago History Museum.

↙

83. Living room with night view simulation, Marina City showroom apartment at 316 West Randolph Street, Bertrand Goldberg Associates, Chicago, IL, 1962. Hedrich-Blessing [photographer]. HB-23215-S, Bertrand Goldberg Archive, Ryerson and Burnham Archives, The Art Institute of Chicago. Courtesy of The Art Institute of Chicago. © The Chicago History Museum

84. A view from balcony into bedroom, Marina City showroom apartment at 316 West Randolph Street, Bertrand Goldberg Associates, Chicago, IL, 1962. Hedrich-Blessing [photographer]. HB-23215-B6, Chicago History Museum.

inhabitants, their presence was implied through casual traces of everyday living. Beyond the window the panorama transformed the city into wallpaper, both literally and figuratively providing a theatrical backdrop for domestic life.

Hedrich-Blessing photographs of the bedroom focus inward. In a typical image taken from the balcony looking in, the space is compressed into an intimate scene. [**Fig. 84**] The bedroom balcony echoed the outdoor room theme; plants along the perimeter, a couple of chairs, and a side table with a journal titled *Living* suggested it as a quiet outdoor reading space. The semi-drawn dark curtains framed a well-lit but again minimal bedroom; the scene's relative austerity is animated by a casually thrown suit jacket lying on the bed.

The showroom linked progress to commerce; it "domesticated" the project's architecture to appeal to consumers without diminishing it. Interior spaces, furnishings, and the panoramic city view placed dramatic new ways of living alongside traditional living patterns. The daring concept of living "high in the sky" was tempered with conventional taste.[15] Regular furniture provided by Chicago's retail giants—Marshall Field's and Carson Pirie Scott and Company—combined with furnishings and objects most likely obtained from the Bordelon Art Gallery. No children's furniture was included, suggesting that the apartments were intended for progressive middle-income individuals and childless couples. The public's general impression, despite minimum FHA space standards, was of spaciousness. Goldberg cited frequent questions about the cost of rentals because the apartments appeared to suggest luxury living.[16]

The showroom's success was undeniable and the public "bought" the idea of Marina City firsthand. Within the first eight months of the showroom opening, applications were received for more than double the available space.[17] And although a special event was held for the Janitors' Union's members and their spouses, BGA also invited bankers and the representatives from the FHA's Washington headquarters to reassure private financiers and federal administrators of their investment.

The Marina City office building was marketed similarly to the apartments. In order to communicate its efficiency, amenities, and spatial clarity to prospective tenants, BGA built a large office interior. The furniture layout was carefully spaced to follow the rhythm of window mullions and to maximize access to natural light, with—once again—a photographic panorama of downtown Chicago. The office showroom's brightness marketed easy access to daylight and good interior lighting—important factors countering occupant fatigue. Like the space, the furniture was light, contemporary, and modular. The office showroom also promoted the idea of the urban workplace next to a resident's home, "living above the store" in the "city within a city."

Hedrich-Blessing's images of the space were made familiar by models posing as secretaries and were used in promotional materials, including the office building rental brochure. [Fig. 85] Here too the uncompromising modernism of the architecture and modular midcentury modern office furniture was tamed by small personal touches. One of the desks was covered with papers, books, an ashtray, and two glass sculptures of horses forming traditional bookends. These photographs were also shot as day and nighttime scenes. Staged within spatial simplicity and efficiency, they too combined familiarity with innovation.

Hedrich-Blessing also took unofficial showroom photos with BGA staff posing in the space, a mark of the office's theatrical humor. One of these shows four men occupying the same space previously used for the official marketing photographs, with two men cleaning the exterior glass facade, the other two pointing to areas to be cleaned. [Fig. 86] The two "window cleaners" appear to be focused on cleaning the glass to perfection—perhaps so that the "paper" Chicago skyline could be that much more believable or to highlight the concrete mullions' effect. The full-scale replica was used for prospective tenants to imagine inhabiting the space and to see its spatial qualities firsthand, as well as for funders, administrators, and politicians to experience the project they patronized.

The Randolph Street show apartments were not the last opportunity to market high-rise living in the Marina City complex. Once the first residential tower was completed, it was equipped with furnished model apartments to aid the rental effort. The model apartments were designed by the Illinois Chapter of the American Society of Interior Designers and included the work of Chicago modernist pioneers like Jody Kingery of Baldwin Kingery. Opened to the public on September 6, 1963, they were included in the hugely popular guided tours of the complex—the *Chicago Daily News* claimed in 1964 that about twelve thousand sightseers took the tour each month.[18]

These model apartments were in many ways an extension of the life-size showroom apartments and offices on Randolph Street.[19] Both strategies combined architectural invention and marketing convention—a specific ambition of BGA that helped prove that "a pie in the sky" was affordable, buildable, marketable, and inhabitable. Hedrich-Blessing documented these model apartments, emphasizing city views, a direct link to the full-scale showroom. Here too the progressive design ideas of Marina City were intentionally diluted by more traditional interior design patterns. Marina City–themed wallpaper in the kitchen provided one example, the frequency of the newest electrical gadgets positioned on traditional furniture another.

The Red and the Silver Books

The marketing of Marina City through publications began with the Groundbreaking Ceremony Brochure, which celebrated its historic legacy and unprecedented scale through an oversized portfolio. But BGA did not stop there; it also produced a series of celebratory and sales-oriented publications about Marina City to support the project's design and promotion. Two square twelve-by-twelve-inch books directed at residential and commercial renters demonstrated Goldberg's early interest and later exposure to bookmaking and graphic design.[20]

The UNEX was Goldberg's inspiration for the one-foot-square format, demonstrating to prospective tenants—residential and commercial—the benefit of the Marina City office building's UNEX value.[21] Encased in white, embossed cardboard slip covers, the brochures were almost identical in appearance. Inside, however, one was red and the other silver with gold endsheets.[22] They advertised Marina City as a bold, heroic, and affordable new urban development. When compared to marketing efforts for an equally historically significant residential complex, Mies's Lakeshore Drive Apartments (1949), Marina City's marketing publications were vastly superior. Their level of detail and finish went also far beyond contemporary parallels, which is interesting given Marina City's low- to middle-income rental market.[23]

The red apartment rental book *Marina City: A City Within a City*, had a slip cover embossed with a typical tower floor plan.[24] It contained descriptions of apartment units and their amenities, a rental application form, diagrams of apartment floor plans, photographs of the showroom apartment, and an over-size folded poster with a photograph of the large-scale model of Marina City. It advertised Marina City as a revolutionary complex, part of a bigger urban strategy—"The McFetridge Plan"—that called for a return to the urban center and its cultural institutions. As a title within the book attested ("Core Concept of High Rise Living"), ideas of social structure were intertwined with structural innovation, the circular structural core representing a social core, a space for encounters, and a symbol of urban density. The red book boldly compared Marina City to other iconic projects, stating that "the construction produces twice the rigidity, for its height, of the Empire State Building."[25] The interior planning aid, developed by BGA and the Marina City Management Corporation, included scaled floor plans of all apartment types and furniture templates for arranging apartment layouts.[26]

The idea of vision and visibility formed a primary marketing and design concept, clearly expressed in a section titled "View from the Heights":

> Whether the season's feature is the color of pleasure craft on the lake or
> river, or the white patterns of snowy roof tops, the Marina City tenant can
> observe the scene from the luxurious comforts of home. And if he cares to
> join any part of the action observed, he can do so quickly and easily, from his
> conveniently centered Marina City base. The option is his; to be a part of—or
> apart from—the city's rich variety at any time.[27]

Highlighting the all-electric lifestyle of Marina City, the book referred to General Electric's appliances and electric heating:

> The exclusive use of electricity for heating makes possible lowest electric rates for conventional purposes—modern lighting, electric blankets, air-conditioning. The probability of stable electricity costs in the future through nuclear and other technological developments in power production, will help keep Marina City rentals at present modest levels. This all-electric city is another Marina City "first" [that is] designed for tenant comfort.[28]

The book also praised Marina City as a genuinely mixed-use development, including sections describing the benefits of the office building, as well as the theater as an entertainment hub bringing the worlds of leisure and show business closer to Marina City tenants. Citing cities of antiquity and the Middle Ages and their works of art and architecture, the book ended with a section devoted to Marina City's concept as a "city within a city." This was illustrated with a map of Chicago, which included Marina City, juxtaposed with a greater area along the Chicago River, and was explained by a short text about its mixed-use features and a list of all the key players in the project: owners, sponsors, lenders, architects, engineers, and contractors.

The office rental marketing brochure, *Marina City: Design for Business*, supported the office leasing effort and was very similar to the red book.[29] Its white slip cover was embossed with the complex's entire plan. The actual silver cover had on it two double-ended arrows representing the UNEX. The office building was marketed as an efficient business space with flexible floor plans adaptable to individual tenants' needs and also as a space connected visually to the city. It included an office planning aid containing a typical floor plan with the location of the vertical core and air-conditioning shafts and an opaque base plan with three tracing sheets on vellum for prospective tenants to test various plan and furniture layouts.[30]

Images of the office showroom emphasized the office building's modernity and efficiency; the silver book also included close-ups of the Marina City model. One of these formed a two-page pop-up spread showing the entire Marina City model. The book also had diagrams showing the UNEX value's ratio and composition, and it highlighted amenities, such as the theater, the four restaurants, the marina, the bowling alley, and the gymnasium, as well as the easy access to downtown's consumer pleasures. A large image of three suited men at lunch presented business as an interplay between work, social interaction, and consumption. This image too was "softened" by recognizable human touches—a breadbasket, half-eaten butter, salt and pepper shakers, cigarette packs, and glasses half-filled with drinks.

Most important, the silver book affirmed the office building as an urban structure. It reminded prospective tenants that their office space would coexist within the Marina City complex's greater context as a hub of urban activity and as a place that derives its value from its proximity to Chicago's cultural institutions, such as the Art Institute of Chicago, the Field Museum, Orchestra Hall, the Chicago Opera House, and the city's various universities.[31] The idea that a true "city within a city" was not a self-sufficient entity permeated the book. The complex offered everything that suburban office parks and residential subdivisions could not: high density, proximity, mixed uses, and culture.

Photographs

From its very beginning Marina City's design, marketing, construction, and publicity efforts were documented through photographs. Numerous photographers were involved, but one firm was most prominent: Hedrich-Blessing. The firm's images circulated so widely in the twentieth century that its name has become synonymous with modern architecture in Chicago and beyond.[32] Founded in 1929 by Ken Hedrich and Hank Blessing, Blessing soon left the firm and Hedrich was joined by his brothers—Ed, Bill, and Jack—forming a unique family operation that later also included their children. The firm also included other photographers and their assistants, such as Bill Engdahl, who took some of the most significant images of Marina City. The firm's early work included Depression-era photographs of important buildings in a stark, sharply contrasting compositional style.

Goldberg used Hedrich-Blessing's services starting in the early 1930s. Bill Hedrich took the 1938 night view of the North Pole Mobile Ice Cream parlor. Since Ken Hedrich photographed the House of Tomorrow, it is likely that Goldberg met Hedrich at Keck and Keck's office. Acting as the de facto official photographers for the Marina City project, Hedrich-Blessing made a powerful contribution to its national and international architectural reputation. Bill Engdahl took one of the most iconic Marina City photographs in 1963 from Lower Wacker Drive; the building's salient features, its ties to Chicago's infrastructure, and its urban character are immediately visible. [Fig. 87]

Robert Sobieszek has argued that the work of Hedrich-Blessing followed general trends in modernist architecture and culture.[33] The highly contrasted, spectacular, and theatrical views of the glittering pavilions of the 1933 Century of Progress exhibition transformed in the 1940s and '50s into subdued shots of buildings by Mies and Albert Kahn. In Marina City's case, Hedrich-Blessing followed the trajectory established in the 1930s, manipulating light to capture the showrooms' dreamy backlighting as well as the glass walls' transparency set against the project's concrete mass. Their approach illustrates Sobieszek's argument that the firm understood each architect's interest in particular materials and forms and tried to capture it through photography.[34] Goldberg, an astute judge of photographs and a capable photographer himself, recognized the skills of the Hedrich-Blessing firm and hired them to document the evolution of Marina City from the very beginning.[35]

Another photographer who took significant images of Marina City was Orlando Cabanban. Unlike Hedrich-Blessing's images, which tried to represent the entire complex, Cabanban focused on detail and inhabitation. A typical Cabanban image of Marina City's balconies highlights the relationship between the two towers. Framed by the curving lines of floor slabs and railings, the image shows a balcony from one residential tower extending the view to the second tower, establishing a visual dialogue within the complex (see Fig. 8).

Richard Nickel, another noted Chicago photographer, also took an iconic Marina City image. In it the Marina City core rises in State Street's perspectival space. The photograph perfectly juxtaposes the tower's heroic engineering with the nineteenth-century city grid, capturing the feel of old Chicago as it was erased to make way for the next generation of its iconic structures. With spectators gazing at the rising core as they go about their everyday business, the image also captures a sense of popular excitement and curiosity among Chicagoans in the early 1960s (see Fig. 48).

→
87. **View with Chicago River and ship passing under upraised bridge in the foreground, Marina City (1959–1967), Bertrand Goldberg Associates, Chicago, IL, ca. 1965.** Bill Engdahl, Hedrich-Blessing [photographer], HB-23215-X2, Chicago History Museum.

Day and Night

Goldberg was also interested in the changing experience of architecture across seasons and day and night. In 1965 he wrote:

> Marina City is a lighted city. The question of the difference of appearance between daytime and nighttime is an important design factor for urban centers—not so much for the suburbs, not so much for the countryside, but in town where people will live with a structure 24 hours a day, the difference in appearance between the structure in summer and winter and day and night becomes a change of tremendous importance.[36]

Thus we find numerous photographs of Marina City by night and day, as well as in summer and winter. A typical example of contrasting night and day photographs was a pair of photos of the commercial platform. The daylight image by an unknown photographer showed boats in the marina with a frozen Chicago River dominated by the parking structure's sharply shadowed helixes. [Fig. 88] The night view by Hedrich-Blessing completely transformed this familiar scene, its glow enhanced by light reflected on the office building's floors and mullions. [Fig. 89]

Light was also used to unify the complex's physical presence. Christmas lights issued to tenants by Marks and Company in the complex's early days were strung along balcony rails, transforming the residential towers into giant Christmas treelike structures. A more artistic long-exposure photograph shows Marina City's lit balconies and their intricate curvilinear geometries. A slowly moving camera distorted the geometry and transformed these into hybrid light trails (see Fig. 65).

The Marina City photographs' dramatic quality—whether day or night views—was further enhanced by their almost classical theatricality. Goldberg's love of theater permeated each project phase, whether design, construction, marketing, or finance. He used theatricality as a didactic tool to enhance the message and to create more familiar and appealing Marina City images for audiences used to movies and television. The carefully constructed settings of the Marina City showroom apartments represented both novelty and familiarity; the office showroom, with BGA "acting-out," was perhaps the most emblematic of Goldberg's sense of theater. Theatricality even penetrated Marina City Management Corporation's *Marina City Newsletter* published in 1964 and 1965 to advertise Marina City's amenities and document notable celebrities' various visits to the complex—such as King Simeon of Bulgaria or actor Gary Lockwood standing on the roof deck and taking pictures of the city below. [Fig. 90] The newsletter extended earlier marketing strategies, aiding the rental efforts and boosting a positive image of the complex, while at the same reinforcing the idea of vision and visibility as one of Marina City's inherent features. The complex was built to be seen from many vantage points in the city—it was a new landmark in the always changing Chicago skyline. Yet, Marina City also acted as a viewing platform—it was a viewing device made of balconies, decks, and raised promenades. It was a gigantic camera from which the image of Chicago was captured, photographed, and reproduced. It was both an object of observation and an observing device.

The complex's architectural elements—towers, theater, and office—also functioned as architectural "actors" on the commercial platform's "podium," this time for an audience across the Chicago River. The two residential towers'

↗
88. Restaurant and marina by day, Marina City (1959–1967), Bertrand Goldberg Associates, Chicago, IL, 1964. Bertrand Goldberg Archive, Ryerson and Burnham Archives, The Art Institute of Chicago. © The Art Institute of Chicago.

→
89. Restaurant and marina by night, Marina City (1959–1967), Bertrand Goldberg Associates, Chicago, IL. Hedrich-Blessing reproduction of a photograph by an unknown artist. HB-41780, Bertrand Goldberg Archive, Ryerson and Burnham Archives, The Art Institute of Chicago. © The Art Institute of Chicago. Courtesy of The Art Institute of Chicago. © The Chicago History Museum

Who could resist the view from a Marina City balcony? King Simeon, like all avid photographers, could hardly wait until the film was developed. These dramatic photos of the skyline will captivate his friends at home.

The frozen food section of Marina City Finer Foods certainly is mouth-watering. Morris H. Swibel, left, talks with Colonel Frank W. Chesrow, president of the Board of Trustees of the Metropolitan Sanitary District of Greater Chicago, while King Simeon and Queen Margarita of Bulgaria look over the variety of foods offered in the supermarket.

Seeing is believing. "It's simply unbelievable that one could have television equipment in one's home," said King Simeon. So he visited the television transmitting studio of the new baby in town, WFLD (UHF Channel 32), on the 19th floor of Marina City. Looking like the proud father is Marina Management's vice president, Morris H. Swibel, and smiling at the right is Queen Margarita.

WHAT'S CURRENT AND CULTURAL?

(As a service to Marina City residents, we present a listing of current cultural events which you may find of interest.)

THE CHICAGO PUBLIC LIBRARY

. . . through April 30th. Photography of Manuel Carillo, one of Mexico's prize-winning photographers. The collection, titled "The Inseparables," deals with the friendship between people and animals and their influence on one another's lives. Carillo's interest in photography began when he saw foreign visitors and tourists taking photographs of the Mexican people. His photographs emphasize the human qualities of the people and their simplicity. The collection can be seen in the first floor exhibition corridor.

ART INSTITUTE OF CHICAGO

. . . Through April 24 in the Morton Wing. "The Matisse Retrospective" is the first complete survey since the artist's death in 1954. The show includes 90 oil paintings, covering all periods, most of the artist's 67 bronzes, an extensive group of drawings and graphics, as well as Matisse illustrations for books. Many of the family pictures have never before been exhibited publicly and many of the pictures from European collections have never before been exhibited in America.

. . . Through May 10. The 26th Annual Exhibition Society for Contemporary Art.

. . . Through May 1. The 69th Annual Exhibition, Artists of Chicago and Vicinity.

. . . Through May 15. Photographs by Danny Lyon.

RENAISSANCE SOCIETY

. . . April 17 through June 12. Contemporary Italian painting and sculpture. Daily 10-5. Saturday 1-5 pm. Goodspeed Hall at the University of Chicago, 1010 East 59th.

CHICAGO HISTORICAL SOCIETY

. . . April 24. "Casablanca" starring Humphrey Bogart, Ingrid Bergman, Claude Rains and Paul Henreid. Sunday, ·2:15 pm. May 1. "The Maltese Falcon" starring Humphrey Bogart, Sidney Greenstreet, Peter Lorre Mary Astor.

NIGHT LIFE

. . . "Joy '66" — a swinging musical revue by Oscar Brown, Jr. Starring Oscar Brown, Jr. and his friends at the Happy Medium, 901 North Rush. Shows nightly

(Continued on page 4)

90. *"Seeing is believing"* – King Simeon
of Bulgaria taking pictures from the
Marina City balcony and admiring the
new Marina City TV station. From *Marina
City Newsletter*, April 1966. Bertrand Goldberg
Archive, Ryerson and Burnham Archives, The Art Institute
of Chicago. © The Art Institute of Chicago.

height and formal exuberance in particular, with the office building backdrop
and the half-hidden, saddle-shaped theater, suggested that architectural form
and urban lifestyle were the main actors in this urban spectacle, with the car a
close second.

Goldberg's handling of Marina City's public relations relied on a sophisticated understanding of message and audience. He felt no qualms in presenting
a square scheme to the FHA to gain mortgage insurance and then showing a
circular one to the client and City of Chicago. Most of the Marina City press
releases were written by Goldberg and almost all of the photography was
orchestrated through his office. The office created the "Hello Chicago" billboard facing the river advertising the project's imminent arrival to the public.
The silver and red books were designed for two different yet equally aspiring
audiences. Within the residential brochure, the interior planning aid allowed
renters to become stage directors. Dramatic perspective renderings lent high
cultural capital to the project. Most important, Goldberg brought the talents of
Hedrich-Blessing and Orlando Cabanban to the project, and their photographs
elevated Marina City to iconic local and international architectural status. These
strategies, appearing in a plethora of professional and entertainment publications, helped the project enter the local and sometimes international popular
consciousness. Marina City's publicity continued well after its completion to
inspire a debate whose local and international voices testified to the broad
reach of Marina City's communication strategies.

chapter six

rewrapping marina city

GOLDBERG HAS BEEN UNFAIRLY STEREOTYPED AS AN ARCHITECT DRAWING CONCLUSIONS TO FIT HIS CIRCLES.... HIS BUILDINGS MAKE SENSE FROM THE STANDPOINT OF ECONOMICS AS WELL AS STRUCTURE. HISTORICALLY, GOLDBERG'S SHELLS AND CURVILINEAR SHAPES ARE HARDLY REVOLUTIONARY. BUT IN A WORLD OF BOXES, THEY DO SEEM SO.

—LINDA LEGNER, "THE GOLDBERG VARIATIONS: SPACE AND STRUCTURE"

Marina City's marketing strategies produced a body of images and texts that traveled across the world. They fed Marina City's power as a physical destination for tourists and architectural critics, who in turn added to its reception within architectural and popular culture. After its completion Marina City was included in a number of Chicago, national, and international exhibitions, as well as in associated catalogs and many independent publications. Goldberg was honored for his work both abroad—in France he received the insignia of *Officier de l'Ordre des Arts et Lettres* (Officer of the Order of Arts and Letters)—and in the United States, where he received many design awards. At the same time, Marina City provoked significant criticism locally as well as, to a lesser extent, further afield.

Marina City's reception was inseparable from the broader urban and cultural discourse of its time, including debate on the city in Europe and Asia. In his writings and interviews, Goldberg often referred to his desire to design communities rather than single structures, which paralleled similar efforts by other architects in the 1960s and '70s. In Japan, the Metabolists' group, which emerged around 1959, the year that Marina City was commissioned, explored similar themes including city growth and the design of large-scale urban communities. These ideas were particularly visible in Kiyonori Kikutake's Marine City Project (1958–1963), which deployed strategies similar to Marina City: circular skyscrapers and the programmatic juxtaposition of urban dwelling with life on the water. [Fig. 92] Kisho Kurokawa's Nagakin Capsule Tower (1972) explored ideas about modular housing and minimum dwellings, as well as ideas about prefabrication and mass production. Like Marina City, the Nagakin Capsule Tower relied on a high-density population and technology in service of urban

←
91. Marina City, from the filming of *The Hunter*. Chicago, IL, 1979. *Chicago Sun-Times*, Charles Kirman [photographer]. Courtesy and by permission of the *Chicago Sun-Times* and Charles Kirman. Bertrand Goldberg Archive, Ryerson and Burnham Archives, The Art Institute of Chicago. © The Art Institute of Chicago.

92. Marine City, Kiyonori Kikutake, view of model c.1963.

93. Marin County Civic Center, Frank Lloyd Wright, San Rafael, CA, 1960–1976.

growth. In his book *Goldberg: Dans la Ville / On the City*, Michel Ragon recognized this project's importance, although he stated that Marina City had already pioneered the idea of a concrete shell attached to a central reinforced core before the Nagakin Tower.

The later work of Frank Lloyd Wright shows many parallels to Goldberg's explorations—in particular in the study of circular form and articulation of large structures. Wright's Marin County Civic Center in San Rafael, California (1960–1976), completed well after the architect's death, explores round form and mixed use, as well as ideas of vision by and visibility of users through the use of balconies, promenades, and internal corridors. [Fig. 93] However, unlike Goldberg's work, Wright's architectural ideas originate not from an urban vision but rather from its link to topography and vegetation—the interrelationship of architecture and landscape.

The work of the United Kingdom–based group Archigram explored similar urban and contextual themes, albeit from a different perspective, focusing on the design of new kinds of communities and the integration of new technology. Archigram's Plug-In City proposal (1964) explored urban ideas based on modular residential units as foundations for communal urban spaces. Like Marina City it presented a vision of the city based on verticality, with a complex system of tubes and cranes used to move goods, on which housing and shopping was also "hung." The connection between Archigram and Goldberg, though formally obvious, needs to be regarded with care, however. Goldberg met Peter Cook for the first time shortly before his death in 1997; one of the coauthors was present at the time. The meeting was cordial and the two men were fascinated by one another, yet both seemed also to be sizing each other up. More important, their design philosophies differed significantly. Archigram projects did not place economy and efficiency as central to their endeavors; thus their formal and programmatic palette was less restricted.

Archigram and the Japanese Metabolists explored modern metropolitan themes shaped by capitalist development, new technologies, and rapid growth. This discourse was a part of a broader debate about the city also visible in the work of groups like Superstudio and others, such as the practice Candilis, Josic, and Woods. Many of their projects relied on the idea of a *megastructure*, a term elaborated by Reyner Banham to describe large-scale, mixed-use urban structures. However, Ragon cautioned that Goldberg's work should not be confused with megastructures and their often-disorienting scale. Ragon wrote, "Bertrand Goldberg never uses the term *megastructure*, because he is wary of it. For him, megastructures like those proposed by the futurology of the sixties are too large. He prefers…to separate the megastructure into sections and create focal points so that people can orient themselves and form clusters of activity."[1] These parallels and differences between Goldberg, Archigram, and the Metabolists are important, particularly as Marina City was one of the few mixed-use skyscraper projects in the world, an important aspect of its wide-spread reception at the time.

Domestic Reception

In the United States, Marina City's reception was both highly enthusiastic and mixed, depending on the venue and audience. The Architectural League of New York awarded Goldberg with a Silver Medal in 1965, and closer to home a part of the Chicago architectural community embraced Marina City with great pride. Goldberg received the Chicagoan of the Year award from the Chicago Junior Association of Commerce and Industry in 1965.[2] In 1967 the Chicago Chapter of the AIA honored Marina City with the Distinguished Building Award and in 1991 followed it with a Twenty-five Year Award.

The Chicago-based magazine *Inland Architect* was a supporter from the beginning, regularly featuring Marina City. The project first appeared in *Inland Architect* in November 1961 as a full-page rendering advertising a light-weight concrete aggregate.[3] By the January 1962 issue, the editors had added monthly construction progress images to the magazine's contents page.[4] These appeared throughout 1962 and early 1963 and included aerial views, views from the river, and close-ups of construction workers. The first, a nighttime photo published in January 1962, shows the first tower rising to just above the parking structure and features a prominent banner advertising Marina City as "a city within a city" and the tallest residential tower in the world. In the February 1962 issue, this image was repeated, the caption capturing the sense of excitement, "Progress of Marina Towers has been a matter of consuming interest for all architects and the editors hope to place a progress photo on this page each month to keep readers abreast of this unusual structure."[5] The quote reflected a common misunderstanding—the entire complex was reduced to "Marina Towers." The caption in the April 1962 issue celebrated Marina City construction crews: "Winter construction involves many problems for both architect and contractor. These billowing tarps show that work at Marina City continues in all weather."[6]

In January 1974, *Inland Architect* published a special four part overview of Goldberg's work. A short essay by Linda Legner titled "The Goldberg Variations: Space and Structure," argued that despite Marina City's favorable publicity Goldberg was still perceived as a somewhat strange and unusual figure among Chicago's architects. Marina City was not featured as one of the projects in the overview but the editors of *Inland Architect* recognized its urban potential: "Marina City…remains remarkable not merely as a structural statement but perhaps more significantly as an urban statement.... Marina City also reaches out into the city at large, although of course it is a security-conscious middle-class preserve and no exemplar of the all-purpose mix that our cities must eventually develop."[7] Marina City as a mixed-use building was also highlighted in *Chicago's Famous Buildings*, a guide to Chicago architecture written by, among others, Ira Bach.[8] Inclusion of Marina City, despite Bach's possible partisanship, marked its quick rise as an iconic Chicago structure.

In 1985 an exhibition titled 150 Years of Chicago Architecture, which included an overview of the city's architecture from the 1830s to the mid-1980s, was held at Chicago's Museum of Science and Industry. The exhibition, initially held in 1983 in Paris, was organized by Ante Glibota, curator of the most comprehensive retrospective of Goldberg's work. Goldberg's role in the exhibit was reviewed and introduced by Allan Temko, the architectural critic for the *San Francisco Chronicle*.[9] "Chicago's finest poets have been architects," said Temko, positioning Goldberg alongside Louis Sullivan, Frank Lloyd Wright, and Mies van der Rohe.[10] Temko also recognized the importance of urbanism in Goldberg's work:

> That diversity is the key to democratic life in huge industrial cities, Goldberg never doubted. Compared to the coercive pigeon-holing of the inmates of Le Corbusier's Unité d'Habitation in Marseilles, France (at the time, the most famous residential megastructure of the modern movement), Marina City— with twice as many residents—is festive and free, especially in fine weather when secretaries and executives, lawyers and school teachers, are out on balconies, enjoying cookouts and views of the loop and the lake.[11]

Yet Marina City was also clearly controversial, particularly in Chicago. In 1962, popular journalists called it "exhibitionist" and some local property owners did not agree with labor acting as property owners.[12] Parallel to populist suspicion was the local architectural community's skepticism. Despite his great admiration for Mies's work, Goldberg was seen as betraying Chicago's most famous adopted "son." In 1954, Herbert Greenwald, in an understandably partisan letter to Mies, repudiated Goldberg for being too ambitious and drawing too much on his connection with Mies.[13] Despite his Bauhaus education, Goldberg continued to be received coolly by Chicago's Miesian circle. When a Bauhaus exhibition came to IIT, Goldberg was not invited to join the advisory board or to contribute work, as might have been expected of a former Bauhaus student. Records exist of only two formal presentations by Goldberg at IIT between 1960 and 1990, with one of these for the Office of Alumni Programs.[14] It appears that he was never quite forgiven for breaking the Miesian ethos of the right angle. This frostiness echoed that accorded to Chicago architects Harry Weese and Walter Netsch whose work also resisted formal categorization within the Miesian architectural idiom.

The complex relationship between Goldberg and Mies acquired a further visible manifestation. One of Chicago's urban legends is that, as Marina City was built, the Miesian camp quickly created a commission for Mies to dwarf Marina City. The result, IBM Plaza (1973), not only rose above Marina City but also helped obscure its visibility from Michigan Avenue. True or not, it is difficult to imagine another city in which two major architects would be given an urban arena in which to enact such controversy. While some critics, like *Inland Architect*'s editors, called the contrast between the two buildings "a handsome relationship," others, like Allan Temko, recognized that contrast as less innocent:

> Whereas the black office building stands aloof in the city, complete in itself as a statement of abstract corporate strength, Goldberg's elating cylindrical towers are virtually lodged in the surrounding urban fabric.[15]

Criticisms of Marina City crossed generational and conceptual divides within the Chicago architectural community. Goldberg was received with skepticism by the subsequent generation of Chicago architects aligned with postmodernism. This was particularly evident in exhibition catalog *150 Years of Chicago Architecture* in which only an addendum, titled "Masters," covered the work of Goldberg, Netsch, and Weese. Furthermore, perhaps intending praise, the editors placed the triad's work in opposition to the city's Miesian tradition as well as its emerging postmodern camp.

Stanley Tigerman wrote an ambiguous response in a postscript titled "Goldberg, Netsch and Weese: In Exile at Home."[16] Though he acknowledged that Marina City was "wonderfully urban" and "structurally inventive," he felt that its towers "never really became the example that one might have thought they could have become—somehow, they seemed too personal and eccentric for the taste of a national architectural community."[17] Here again Marina City was reduced to its residential program and its iconic form. Tigerman saw Goldberg as one of "three native Chicagoans swimming upstream; struggling against the current; detached from their origins by the spirit of an age."[18] Applauding Goldberg's departure from Miesian modernism, Tigerman nevertheless could not accommodate Goldberg's "difference." Later, in Goldberg's obituary, he was quoted as saying about Marina City, "At the level of picture postcards for visitors, they are great, but at the functional level, the pie shape is the reverse of what it needs to be."[19]

Tigerman's words emerged from Chicago's architectural debate of the 1970s and '80s. An earlier 1976 exhibition at the Museum of Contemporary Art titled 100 Years of Architecture in Chicago had resulted in a second exhibition—a kind of *salon des refusés*. Titled Chicago Architects, it featured the work of lesser-known architects opposing the Miesian canon. Its catalog included Goldberg's work (but only his 1930s projects) as well as Tigerman's.[20] With hindsight it is easy to imagine that both men would have felt uncomfortable about being included in the same category.

A variation on the Chicago Architects show was organized in Verona, Italy, in 1981. In its catalog *Beyond the International Style: New Chicago Architecture*—containing essays supportive and critical of Goldberg's work—Christian Norberg-Schulz, another postmodern critic, wrote a critical response in which he saw Marina City's departure from Chicago's tartan grid as a rejection of its genius loci. He wrote, "Freely shaped buildings such as the round late-modern *Marina City Towers*, look foreign in Chicago."[21] Although he promoted postmodern architects employing abstract classicism such as Helmut Jahn and Tom Beeby, it is surprising that he paid little attention to Marina City's plaza—a civic space with a rich history of precedents.[22]

Goldberg's Response

Goldberg reacted to the Marina City criticism in lectures, interviews, and essays that elaborated the ideas behind the project and explained his broader intellectual interests. He grounded Marina City in ideas about urbanity and civic life. Referring to Lewis Mumford's reflections on the history of urbanism, Goldberg saw the city as a cultural and economic construct similar to the medieval city-state. With its civic plaza, Marina City contributed to this ideal:

> We have created a plaza in the best European classical sense of the city square, and on the plaza we have erected five interrelated buildings....The plaza becomes the open platform on which automobiles and people, alternately passengers and pedestrians can wander as they choose.[23]

Similar concerns were explored in Goldberg's essays "Rich is Right," and "The Critical Mass of Urbanism," both originally published in *Inland Architect*. "Rich is Right" despite its somewhat ironic title, presented a clear argument against postmodernism, an "infection" that he also called "trendy garbage."[24] Although he called architecture "a social art in an industrial age," he was critical of architectural modernism's "right angle society," suggesting instead a role for architects based on humanism.[25] "The Critical Mass of Urbanism" focused on urbanity and the architect's role as its steward.[26] As the title suggests, the key was the preservation of urban density, which, according to Goldberg, was defined as "that number of people which creates the human fission and fusion we call communication, which in turn established community."[27] Goldberg was aware that these issues transcended traditional functionalist and pragmatic models of design, planning, and politics. He wrote, "25 years after Marina City, I suspect that the real issue of urban architecture remains this tension, perhaps even this struggle, to identify fact and faith and the role of the architect in each."[28] According to Goldberg the struggle between fact and faith dominated the twentieth century, often resulting in extreme views. In his work, he tried to reconcile the two—faith and fact, the ideal and the real.

Goldberg also recognized the failure of planners' efforts to save the city—a residue of nineteenth-century blind technocratic rationalism:

> We also must ask a question of our governments about the spiritual destiny of cities: can we through government action, stop the decay of humanistic values of our cities? Can we self-consciously restore the city as a center of community and mystery of human warmth and spirit? I believe yes, but not yet. There will be a long delay. These values can be restored only when governments believe in humanism and believe that the city can be its shelter. Perhaps the architects first must believe, as Vitruvius warned, that they must know more about the government than the king. Perhaps then the architects can teach the king.[29]

He saw the architect as a facilitator of social goals working closely with government and private capital to enhance the public good. These ideals were sometimes closer to architects in places where modernism remained more closely aligned with the social program of the welfare state.

International Reception
Goldberg's work received far more attention and praise abroad than at home— likely the result of his ongoing participation in the transatlantic exchange of ideas. His Bauhaus education created an early foundation for international dialogue and his circle of friends and acquaintances included important international architects, critics, and artists.[30] Goldberg's office also employed

architects and engineers from the United Kingdom in the 1950s and '60s such as Frank Newby and David Dunster.

International articles about Marina City were published in Canada, England, France, Germany, Italy, Poland, and Sweden, among others; only a few of these are reviewed here. In June 1965, Arena: The Architectural Association Journal published a review of contemporary American housing, by William Allen, the principal of the Architectural Association School of Architecture, which included Marina City.[31] In 1967, Arena published an essay by Richard MacCormac titled "Notes on the Role of Form in the Design Process" that included Goldberg's Marina City alongside James Stirling's history library at Cambridge University—one of the most important and controversial buildings of the time.[32] "The solution was remarkably elegant," said MacCormac, and the article included a dramatic view of Marina City.[33] Reyner Banham, the most important British architectural historian and theorist of Goldberg's generation, suggested that Marina City was a sketch for a possible third phase in the history of the Chicago School. Even though these were relatively short references, such appreciation speaks about Marina City's swift rise to iconic international status.

Architectural critic Heinrich Klotz published a comprehensive overview of Goldberg's work in a July 1975 issue of Architecture and Urbanism, where he stressed the importance of Goldberg's urban vision.[34] He revisited Marina City in his essay titled "The Chicago Renaissance" included in Beyond the International Style: New Chicago Architecture where he called Marina City (towers) "the most convincing and impressive arguments against Mies…They stand out in this city like exclamation marks against the domination of the box, they alone challenge the neatly tied-up packages of space which almost exclusively determine Chicago's cityscape."[35] He claimed that "since Mies and Goldberg, nothing much had happened" in Chicago.[36] He was also critical, perceiving Marina City as "stuck" between modernism and postmodernism, lacking "narrative character."[37] Yet he also wrote that Goldberg's buildings "had kept the touch of pure architecture"; he quoted Robert Venturi as saying that they had remained "explicit heroic architecture."[38]

Goldberg's work was particularly visible in Europe during the Parisian run of the 150 Years of Chicago Architecture exhibition in 1983, in which his work was prominently featured as an example of Chicago's "innovative upward motion."[39] The show traveled to La Rochelle, Toulouse, and Zagreb prior to its 1985 Chicago run.[40] Also in 1985, Ante Glibota organized a retrospective exhibition of Goldberg's work at the Paris Art Center, accompanied by the book Goldberg: Dans la Ville / On the City, edited by Michel Ragon, which remains the most comprehensive account of Goldberg's work to date.[41]

The book is a compendium of essays and projects, illustrated with many iconic photographs of Goldberg's buildings. Glibota wrote a short preface positioning Goldberg in the history of Chicago architecture as "the successor to the innovative spirit of Jenney, Sullivan, and others of the Chicago School. His works attracted critical and public attention in Paris and in other European cities."[42] Ragon also placed Goldberg alongside heroes of architectural modernism such as Kenzo Tange, Eero Saarinen, Jørn Utzon, Félix Candela, and Louis Sullivan. He wrote that Goldberg "is undoubtedly, since Sullivan, the most Chicagoan of the Chicagoans. Marina City has become an emblem of Chicago, like the Eiffel Tower in Paris."[43] Ragon saw Goldberg's urban emphasis in opposition to Frank Lloyd Wright and Mies van der Rohe, whom he saw as "anti-urbanists."[44]

Despite Goldberg's assertions that he was an attentive student of Mies, Ragon wrote that "Marina City totally contradicted Mies' work. Not only by its form, in which the curve 'thumbed its nose' at the right angle, but also by its material (concrete instead of steel)....The disciple revolts."[45] According to Ragon, concrete allowed Goldberg to create spaces inspired by natural shell forms.

This fluidity of form was one of the main reasons for Goldberg's departure from Miesian architecture. Goldberg said:

> When I became the first to oppose Mies and to try to create work which was in contradiction with his, my colleagues thought I'd gone crazy. Mies didn't understand that I was building Marina City with the same logic as his boxes, while discovering another space and greater economy. I was revolting against a century of static space, against the straight line, against the idea of man made in the image of the machine...it seemed to me that Mies was not an urbanist, but rather an anti-urbanist.[46]

Ragon was particularly intrigued by Goldberg's commitment to democracy, which he saw as typically American, linking Thomas Jefferson's ideas with Louis Sullivan's architecture. Ragon lamented that Goldberg hadn't built anything outside the United States, despite the universal nature of his thinking, which focused on common issues of every culture—habitat and health.[47]

Alvin Boyarsky, later the chairman of the Architectural Association School of Architecture in London, promoted Marina City in the 1960s and '70s when writing about Chicago architecture while serving as the associate dean of the College of Architecture and the Arts at the University of Illinois at Chicago Circle. In January 1966 he was interviewed by Richard Hoffmann for *Chicago's American Magazine* in an article titled "Chicago: Study in Power and Clarity."[48] Conceived as a walking tour of Chicago's Central Business District, the article was a collection of Boyarsky's remarks about Chicago's famous buildings. Speaking about Boyarsky's assessment of Marina City, Hoffmann said, "The twin cylindrical spires of Marina City visible from Boyarsky's vantage point appeared to him to 'read well among the crisp vertilineal geometry of the Chicago style.'"[49]

In December 1970, Boyarsky published "Chicago a la Carte—The City as an Energy System" in which he constructed Chicago's urban history based on official and unofficial visual records, including popular picture postcards and newspaper clippings.[50] He praised the city's infrastructural works and its "second nature," calling O'Hare Airport "Versailles to Chicago."[51] He was critical of post-Miesian neoclassical tendencies that served corporate interests and eroded public space.[52] The only positive example, the Marina City complex, occupied two full pages in his essay. It was represented by an unusual gritty view "from the back" showing railroad tracks, elevated streets, cars, and warehouses, capturing the seediness of the old River North area, with the Marina City complex rising above as a symbol of new architecture. The next page contained a collage of Marina City images, showing its balconies, the theater building with its graceful curved glass corner, the commercial platform as it touched the river, and a Marina City postcard.

According to Boyarsky, Marina City's "'village green' and extraordinary section so nicely captures the ambience of the place and gives some direction for the future."[53] He resisted the seduction of its towers and recognized it as an urban complex, acknowledging its mixed-use program. He wrote:

The aptness, wit and general city-building sense of Marina City Variations on the Podium Tower Scheme…reveals in it the grittiness and complexity of Chicago's multilayered infrastructure, all the while winking back at the miniaturized twin towers of 860 and 880 Lake Shore Drive, and…goes out of its way to extend the public realm and demonstrate a possible way for rebuilding the frontage along the Chicago River.[54]

For Boyarsky Marina City was the opposite of George Schipporeit's Lake Point Tower (1968), fenced in by a tall brick wall, or the Daley Plaza (1967), where a large steel Picasso sculpture prevented people from gathering. The essay highlighted another important aspect of Marina City: its ability to excite both architects and the public, with the postcard acting as a testament.

Marina City in Construction Journals and Popular Media

The success of Marina City as an icon was evident in a reverse process of appropriation by the construction industry and within popular culture. Its structural, technical, and constructional innovations were quickly picked up by the construction industry. Images of the complex appeared on journal covers for the concrete industry, electrical companies, and many other areas of construction expertise. Various construction trades and material manufacturers appropriated Marina City images—from stair builders to the makers of lightweight concrete aggregates.[55] An Italian cement industry brochure featured a dramatic worm's eye view of the complex on its cover. [Fig. 94] General Electric included Marina City in its 1964 Annual Report, showing a nighttime view of the complex wrapped in Christmas lights. [Fig. 95] In 1965, the Portland Cement Company made a film titled *This is Marina City*, which documented the feat of its construction in great detail.

Commonwealth Edison (Com Ed) in particular used Marina City for its advertising—the phrase "city within a city" was useful in convincing the public about the benefits of flameless heating and cooking. A January 1963 Com Ed advertisement published in *Inland Architect* called Marina City: "So Clean. So Safe. So Modern." and presented Marina City's as the best in modern living with its easy environmental control and cleanliness.[56] This was also evident in another Com Ed advertisement showing a woman speaking on the phone in a Marina City kitchen with an electric stove, a dishwasher, and other equipment, which made it look like an airplane cockpit.[57] [Fig. 96]

Images of Marina City in printed media, films, and commercial clips built upon the theatrical and heroic quality of official brochures and showrooms, as well as other promotional materials prepared by Goldberg. The complex was also featured in Chicago and foreign travel brochures and for a time became one of the most popular postcards of Chicago. [Fig. 97] In 1962, Marina City was featured in *Fortune* magazine in an essay by Gilbert Cross titled "The House the Janitors Built" in which he wrote, "The most exciting feature of the Chicago skyline today is a pair of tall, slim towers, rising like immense pagodas, out of what has long been a dingy neighborhood of warehouses and bars north of the Chicago River."[58] This text highlighted Marina City's metaphorical quality—its ability to inspire the public imagination. Its design was both unique and ambiguous enough to allow for different interpretations—corncobs, pagodas, rockets—which contributed to Marina City's iconic presence and the affection with which it was regarded by the Chicago public.

94. *L'industria Italiana del cemento*,
brochure cover, 1969. By permission of
L'industria Italiana del cemento. Bertrand Goldberg
Archive, Ryerson and Burnham Archives, The Art Institute
of Chicago. © The Art Institute of Chicago.

95. *General Electric Annual Report*, **cover,**
1964. By permission of General Electric Co. Bertrand
Goldberg Archive, Ryerson and Burnham Archives, The Art
Institute of Chicago. © The Art Institute of Chicago.

A magnificent view outside . . . sheer comfort inside. Because with just the flick of a thermostat, you can get the exact temperature you want in any room . . . thanks to Flameless Electric Heat. The radiant baseboard (beneath window) is your main source of heat. Unit above door at left acts as a heat booster, doubles as an air conditioner.

Chicago River and Marina City

Bedrooms are spacious, with balconies overlooking the skyline. Each bedroom has its own thermostat. You can set heat to give you the daytime or sleeping temperature that you want.

The bathroom has a switch-controlled, fan-type heating unit in the ceiling. Boosts heat instantly so you never feel chilled when you step out of a bath.

The modern Marina City kitchens are all-electric, of course. (How else could they be really modern?) With a Flameless Electric Range, your kitchen stays clean longer and at least 10 degrees cooler because the oven is insulated on all six sides. The electric refrigerator is a big 11.8 cubic feet. An electric disposer takes care of the garbage problem. Dishwasher is optional. Individual electric water heater for each apartment (not visible) has control for selecting the water temperature you want.

Get your money's worth with ☰ | ELECTRIC HEAT | **...it's flameless**

96. Marina City, *Commonwealth
Edison Company (ComEd),*
brochure, ca. 1966.

97. Marina City postcard, reprinted
in Alvin Boyarsky, "Chicago a la
Carte," 1970.

Chicago's **Sunday AMERICAN Magazine** MAY 1, 1966

Chicago in the round—
a fresh look at our city

Are there killers in your garden?

The new prom fashions are eye catchers

The complex also appeared on many cover pages of popular magazines, including the 1966 cover for the *Chicago's Sunday American* magazine. [**Fig. 98**] In June 1967 Marina City appeared on *National Geographic*'s cover in a fish-eye view of the riverbank by night, the unique geometry emphasized by Christmas lights on almost every balcony—a recognizable image already featured on the 1964 *General Electric Annual Report* cover.[59] In the accompanying article "Illinois—The City and the Plan," *National Geographic* endorsed the project as a synonym for urbanity, confirming its original architectural concept to a broad lay audience.[60] Within the article an image of the complex with people dancing on one of the balconies was captioned: "With the city for footlights, sky-dancers twirl 52 stories high at Marina City. At this height, traffic tumult fades to silence, and the view ranges into Indiana."[61]

Marina City also became a symbol of speed and travel, appearing on airline posters by United Airlines, American Airlines, TWA (Trans World Airlines), and Aeroflot. In 1965, United Airlines released a poster with a colorfully painted view of Marina City's towers dominating the scene.[62] Painted by Tom Hoyne, this poster was developed as a classical painting showing two tourists in the foreground and a boat passing Marina City. This was not the first time that United Airlines had used images of prominent buildings for its marketing. In 1955, Stan Galli designed a poster with a close-up view of Mies van der Rohe's Lake Shore Drive apartments.[63] In a similar spirit, an American Airlines poster featured a painted image of Marina City set against a playfully painted sky and said, "Enjoy an American Holiday in Chicago." [**Fig. 99**]

A colorful 1977 brochure by Aeroflot, the Russian airline (at that time Soviet Airlines) featured a color photograph of the Marina City complex paired with a drawing of a vintage airplane crossing the Atlantic—a reference to Charles Lindbergh's pioneering transatlantic journey in his *Spirit of St. Louis*.[64] This metaphor of change and speed was also used by the car industry. A Ford Motor Company advertisement published in a May 1963

99. Advertisement, American Airlines, ca. 1966. By permission of American Airlines. Bertrand Goldberg Archive, Ryerson and Burnham Archives, The Art Institute of Chicago. © The Art Institute of Chicago.

100. Wilco, *Yankee Hotel Foxtrot*, CD cover, 2002.

→
101. "Corny, but…", *Chicago Daily News*, October 2, 1962.

issue of *Inland Architect* collages a Ford car into a Marina City rendering. The caption said, "The only car that's changed as much as Chicago! Solid, silent, super torque..."[65]

With the resurgence of Chicago's urban culture in the late 1990s, Marina City reappeared as a popular icon of urbanity and modernity. In 2002, an album cover for the Chicago-based rock band Wilco, *Yankee Hotel Foxtrot*, featured an image of Marina City.[66] [Fig. 100] An image of a yellow sky is interrupted by a black and white image of the top of Marina City's towers. The curvilinear grid of balcony overhangs is highlighted in various tones of gray, reflecting the balconies' play of light and shadow. Use of Marina City imagery in popular music also involved an appearance on Def Leppard's *High 'n' Dry* (1981).

Popular representations of Marina City also included humorous reflections. A cartoon in the *Sunday Tribune* by Rowland Emett, a visiting English artist, pictured the two residential towers as two stacks of pancakes.[67] The complex was also represented as two corncobs in an affectionate photograph by Luther Joseph titled "Corny, but..." published in the *Chicago Daily News* in 1962, a metaphor with which Marina City is still associated today.[68] [Fig. 101] Marina City also inspired a series of ephemera including spoons, special police badges, whisky bottles, and so on. Both metaphorical and whimsical, these collectibles adopted Marina City themes, providing yet another bridge between high architecture and consumer culture.

Marina City and Film

Marina City lent itself easily to the dynamism of the moving image. Already during its construction, it had been photographed in series, prefiguring filmic sequences. It had also been in a publicity film for Portland Cement. And with its complex geometry, it thrived on the multiplicity of viewpoints and perspectives offered by film.

This was particularly visible in the representation of Marina City in Philip Kaufman's *Goldstein* (1964), an independent, low-budget, black and white film influenced by French New Wave Cinema. The complex first appears in a dramatic worm's eye view of the towers, followed by a swirling car ride up the Marina City parking ramp. As the four characters in the car cope with the dizziness of the fast ride, images of Marina City columns and the Chicago skyline alternate in the background. The characters reemerge in one of Marina City's central hallways and enter an apartment. Soon, a shocking scene unfolds: two men, a doctor and his assistant, perform an abortion on a woman lying in the middle of a Marina City living room. In the meantime, the fourth man stands on the balcony, smoking and gazing at the city skyline. Laced with black humor, the scene evolves through a series of shots that combine medical equipment and architecture: a physician holding the speculum, a woman crying, a view of the balcony and the Chicago skyline. The scene concludes with characters disappearing into the apartment tower's dimmed circular corridor.

Marina City also appeared in Arthur Penn's *Mickey One* (1965), another cult movie influenced by the French New Wave. The main character, Mickey, a stand-up comedian—played by Warren Beatty—stalked by the mob, flees Detroit for Chicago. As he looks for safety, various Chicago views unfold, including some of Marina City. One of the scenes opens with a dramatic nighttime view of Marina City. At the skating rink, "The Artist"—played by Kamatari Fujikawa—orchestrates a special installation piece, a combination of musical and constructivist effects culminating in spectacular fireworks and the installation's destruction. A Chicago Fire Department truck enters the scene and extinguishes the fire by covering the entire Marina City skating rink with foam.

The other Marina City scene in *Mickey One* is more subtle. It begins with Mickey knocking on an apartment door, quickly entering the apartment, and engaging another character in an argument. In one shot, Mickey is in the foreground with the other character behind him, both framed by the apartment's glass facade, with the balcony overhang and a night view of the city in the distance. As in the nighttime images of the Marina City showroom, the city skyline is visible, albeit as an abstract web of glittering lights and neon signs. In contrast, the interior of the apartment is well lit by several lamps, almost exactly as in the showroom. As Mickey leaves the apartment and enters the parking ramp, a large neon sign that says "Seay & Thomas Real Estate" is visible in the background. That very same Chicago real estate firm would be hired twenty-four years later to sell the commercial property at Marina City.

Marina City was also represented in popular films. Steve McQueen's last movie, *The Hunter* (1980), features the complex prominently. The Marina City scene opens with the camera slowly rising, emphasizing the towers' height. A crime suspect enters the parking structure on foot and steals a car. Followed by McQueen's character in a tow truck, the suspect speeds up the ramp, eventually losing control and diving into the Chicago River. The fall was filmed from three different angles, with Marina City in the background (see Fig. 91). The scene concludes with a worm's eye view of the towers and McQueen standing on the ramp's edge, framed by curvilinear grid of Marina City's balconies. The filming took place on Friday, September 21, 1979, and was viewed by many spectators lined along the river who recorded it in many photographs.

The scene was reenacted in a 2006 Allstate car insurance commercial produced by the Leo Burnett advertising agency, located just across the river from Marina City.[69] The commercial pays homage to two iconic action movies—*The French Connection* (1971) and *The Hunter* (1980). The commercial starts in downtown Chicago where police officers are chasing a suspect under the "El" tracks on Lake Street between Wabash and La Salle streets—a reference to *The French Connection*. The suspect then drives into the Marina City parking structure pursued by the police officers—a reference to the scene from *The Hunter*. As with the original, the scene starts with a quick worm's eye view of the towers and concludes with the car falling into the river, with Marina City once again clearly visible in the background.

The Allstate stunt was covered extensively in the Chicago press. On Monday, October 16, 2006, a day after the filming, the *Chicago Sun-Times* featured an article and photographs of the car plunging into the river.[70] "Does this happen all the time in Chicago?" asked James Dando, a tourist from Toronto, in a *Chicago Tribune* article. "It's just something you don't see every day."[71] Here, the spectacular event was recaptured endlessly—from official cameras to unofficial records made by cell phones and digital cameras, reminding us of Marina City's iconic status and its ability to bridge various forms of representation and entertainment—from films to commercials and personal cell-phone snapshots.

Afterimage

Marina City epitomized the merger of media and architecture that gained unprecedented momentum in the twentieth century. In her book *Privacy and Publicity: Modern Architecture and Mass Media*, Beatriz Colomina examined the construction of modern architecture through mass media and proposed that "the building is, after all, a 'construction' in all senses of the word."[72] She argued that modern architecture became truly modern when it was represented by mass media, suggesting a blurry boundary between image production and the public reception of buildings. Marina City is a textbook example of that relationship.

Popular images of Marina City speak about its relationship to Chicago. Initially, Marina City's "fathers" used Chicago as wallpaper for the showroom balcony. Later, popular culture appropriated Marina City as a metaphor for Chicago. Goldberg's press releases highlighted Marina City's technological innovations, defining Marina City as a metaphor for speed and technology, which influenced its appearances in advertisements. Consuming these images, the public was mesmerized by the residential towers' sheer beauty, scale, and form, often reducing the Marina City concept to its residential component. Goldberg repeatedly argued against such simplification, always returning to Marina City's initial premise—"a city within a city." Reducing the complex only to its iconic towers—the "Marina City Towers" or "Corn on the Cob" as they were often called—for a long time obscured Marina City's urban and social mandate.

After Marina City

Architectural and popular reception of Marina City helped transform Bertrand Goldberg Associates into a nationally and internationally recognized architectural firm. The practice expanded enormously during the project's design and construction. Goldberg saw it as a test case leading to similar developments. Yet none of the planned projects based on the Marina City concept were built. The "second" three-tower Marina City proposal of 1962 did not materialize. Marina City Detroit, a forty million dollar, 450-unit residential tower and 300-unit motel complex, endorsed by Walter P. Reuther, president of the United Automobile Workers Union, was also never realized. The Park City Denver project of 1963 and the 1967 River Park project for Philadelphia remained sketches. Much later in his career, Goldberg also made a design proposal for a Marina City–inspired scheme for the Lake Shore Drive Grand Apartments, also not realized.

Soon after Marina City, however, he completed another important mixed-use housing project, commissioned by Swibel while he was still CHA chairman. Hilliard Homes (1966) comprised two sixteen-story circular concrete towers for the elderly, flanked by two eighteen-story, curvilinear, low-income residential blocks. [Fig. 102] Here too Goldberg wanted to avoid the stigma of boxes; the curvilinear plan created structural and functional efficiencies but more importantly affirmed CHA residents as deserving of similar design attention as middle-income Marina City tenants. With 756 residential units, lawns, playgrounds, and an open-air theater, Hilliard Homes formed a more modest version of Marina City's mixed-use program.

After Hilliard Homes, Goldberg's office built River City, another important mixed-use housing project in Chicago. [Fig. 103] It was to be the culmination of Goldberg's urban housing vision, a true "city within a city." Conceived in the late 1960s, economic and political pressures delayed and transformed its original vision. Design work began in earnest only in the mid-1970s when Goldberg proposed a system of triads of residential towers, each seventy-two stories high and connected every sixteen floors by an aerial walkway. The complex was to be mixed-use, containing schools, shopping centers, office and retail spaces, as well as public and semipublic spaces for residents and guests.

→

102. Raymond Hilliard Homes (1964–1966), Bertrand Goldberg Associates, Chicago, IL, 1966. Orlando Cabanban [photographer]. Ryerson and Burnham Archives, The Art Institute of Chicago. Digital File #200203.081229-158 © The Art Institute of Chicago.

103. River City (c. 1969–1989), Bertrand
Goldberg Associates, Chicago, IL, 1985.

104. Northwestern University Psychiatric
Institute, Prentice Women's Hospital
and Maternity Center (1962–1988),
Bertrand Goldberg Associates, Chicago,
IL. Hedrich-Blessing [photographer]. HB-39160-I.
By permission of the Chicago History Museum.

The city's concerns about density, however, led to the denial of a zoning variance and by the time the project was completed, River City II (ca. 1986) had become a midrise, sinuous, fifteen-story curve of apartments along the Chicago River—the towers "unfolded and laid out" horizontally on their end. The 446-unit complex included one- and two-bedroom apartments, two- and three-bedroom town homes, and three- and four-bedroom penthouses linked by River Walk, a skylit, private interior street. Like its precedent, River City had a marina along the Chicago River and the newest technologies, including closed-circuit television and broadband coaxial cable for distance education.[73] However, it neither had Marina City's richness of detail nor was met with the same excitement by Chicagoans or the international community. Richard J. Daley had died in 1976, the oil crisis had led to a downturn in the Loop's economic fortunes, and postmodernism had arrived in Chicago and international architectural circles; the city held neither the same attraction for real estate investment nor the same role in international architectural culture.

Marina City also foreshadowed a long career for BGA in healthcare facilities. Carefully analyzing nurse-patient relationships, Goldberg developed spatial clusters organized as centripetal, and sometimes radial, forms that balanced patients' privacy with better visibility and care of patients. The plan core contained central nurse stations and support areas with easy access to all four subgroups, each with its own nursery. Hospitals based on these principles were built in Chicago, Boston, Phoenix, Tacoma, and Mobile. A key example, the Prentice Women's Hospital (1974) for Chicago's Northwestern University, comprised a rectilinear base and a quatrefoil bed tower of monolithic concrete-shell construction. [Fig. 104] Formally resembling Marina City, the bed tower exterior shell was cantilevered from the core, providing plan flexibility below. Innovative in programming and structure, the Prentice Women's Hospital pioneered the use of computers to determine building structure, plumbing, work schedules, and accounting; in 1975 it received an award from the *Engineering News-Record* magazine for structural innovation.[74] However, none of these later projects generated the visibility and recognition associated with Marina City.

epilogue

WHAT HAD OCCURRED WAS THE DEPRESSION, AND THE DEPRESSION WAS OUR FORETASTE OF WAR. A RESTUDY OF OUR VALUE SYSTEM — THE SUPERFICIAL NONSENSE, THE STYLE, THE DECORATION OF THE TWENTIES, EVEN IN ITS SO-CALLED MODERN FORMS AT THAT TIME...THE SWEEPING AWAY OF THESE THINGS AND THE SUBSTITUTION OF WHAT IS INDUSTRIALIZED, THE PREFABRICATION OF HOUSING, AND THE SEEKING OF SIMPLICITY IN THE USE OF MORE NATURAL MATERIALS. ALL OF THAT WAS A MIRROR OF THE SOCIAL REVOLUTION THAT WAS OCCURRING, WHICH IN TURN WAS A MIRROR OF THE ECONOMIC FAILURES THAT WE HAD GONE THROUGH AND THE ECONOMIC REEVALUATIONS WE WERE HAVING AT THAT TIME.

—BERTRAND GOLDBERG, *ORAL HISTORY*

Commissioned by a trade union, Marina City grew into a powerful example of a public/private partnership and, over the long-term, an important model for social mobility, urban revitalization, fiscal creativity, and architectural and engineering innovation. It adjusted social ideals to fit a market economy—embracing capitalism for the common man. The project also underlined the centrality of individual, social, and institutional relationships to the success of large-scale architectural and urban endeavors. For a labor union, a realtor, and an architect to engage the most powerful twentieth-century U.S. mayor, realize the largest real estate deal in the Midwest, finance the first and largest federally insured downtown housing project, construct the tallest concrete structure in the world, and fully let its apartments—to create a building which stood as a model for future downtown revival and of the city itself—was an unprecedented achievement. At the same time, Marina City showed the fallibility of individuals and organizations, the tensions between them and the impossibility of even powerful partnerships to anticipate broader economic and political change.

Although Marina City fell victim, for a time, to financial problems and poor management—reflecting the vulnerability of the built environment to market forces—its recent reemergence as a Chicago icon attests to the longevity of its original vision of urbanity, which also represented the American nation itself. In the sky, on the water, in its offices, retail spaces, and the theater, Marina City's mixed-use program showcased upward mobility—a stage for the janitors' investment in a middle-class urban lifestyle that reflected the blue-collar empowerment of postwar America.

Chicago at the time was a kingmaker in U.S. politics. Richard J. Daley was said to be able to deliver the democratic vote to any democratic president,

←
105. Towers at dusk, Marina City (1959–1967), Bertrand Goldberg Associates, Chicago, IL, ca. 1965. Hedrich-Blessing [photographer]. HB-23215-C5, Chicago History Museum.

with McFetridge a key player in the process.[1] Daley intended Marina City to serve his urban and political vision to advance the city's stature within the nation. Yet Marina City also signaled the crisis of the Chicago political machine. McFetridge's replacement by Sullivan, after decades of Chicago leaders, and the move of the Janitors' Union national headquarters from Chicago to Washington, D.C., under Sullivan's leadership, formed important signs of the change. The "machine" was further weakened after Daley's death in 1976, foreshadowing the waning of blue-collar power in the 1970s and '80s. Continental Illinois Bank's collapse in 1984 and the Savings and Loan crisis in the 1980s and '90s exemplified the fragility of the free market economy. If in Marina City, for a time, the "devil" of capitalism won over the "angel" of the common man, this was part of a broader pattern of change.

Marina City also operated on another global stage—that of the Cold War. Conceived two years after Sputnik's entry into space, Marina City's residential towers could be compared to two rockets ready for launch—one reason perhaps for its popularity with tourists.[2] Its spaces emphasized verticality, reaching up and into the "vast void" of the sky. In this context Marina City's technological innovations were also ideological—the tallest concrete structures, the highest residential buildings, the fastest elevators, all-electric apartments, a car space and a boat dock for every resident, as well as a television in every room, all promoted technologies and amenities available to capitalist citizens. Middle-income America could sleep more easily in its lofty apartment, sure of its technological supremacy and superior lifestyle in an age when the world could end at the touch of a finger.

Histories: Europe, America, Midwest

Goldberg's ability to learn from history was somewhat atypical of modernists of the period. He was fluent in European and American architectural history and the history of their ideas. Goldberg was both a student of culture and a student of architecture. He studied the European labor movement, but he had also studied the historical development of round buildings, from the Temple of Diana (1789) by Antonio Asprucci in Rome to I. M. Pei's helical apartment project (1949, unbuilt).[3] The impact of the Middle Ages, and in particular the influence of the rose window and gothic cathedral vault, were also important.

At the other end of the historical spectrum, the impact of the European artistic and architectural avant-garde on Marina City was undeniable, whether directly through Goldberg's Bauhaus studies, or indirectly through his work and contacts. In architecture, Mies of course, but also Ludwig Hilberseimer, were important European influences. In art, Albers informed his exploration of primary form and helped him move beyond a palette of primary colors. Lillian Florsheim's work as an artist and sculptress, itself influenced by Europeans such as Hugo Weber, Goerges Vantongerloo, Naum Gabo, and Max Bill, also impacted his work. Beyond art and architecture, he was also close to a number of leading European cultural figures. Among others, Margot Fonteyn and Rudolf Nureyev attended the opening of Maxim's restaurant at the base of the Astor Tower, and the film director Michelangelo Antonioni stayed at the Goldberg home.[4]

In the United States, Midwestern architectural sources, in particular Sullivan, Wright, and Fuller, and experience of construction management, finance, and marketing, formed a major influence on Marina City. The integration of social program with formal abstraction formed the European influence. With respect to architectural technology, a similar balance of European and

Midwestern influences occurred. Goldberg's time at the Bauhaus and with Mies van der Rohe, Keck and Keck, Howard T. Fisher and Paul Schweikher, his exposure to R. Buckminster Fuller, and his work on projects like Unicel and Unishelter directed him to modular design, prefabrication, the study of material and environmental systems, and construction sequencing and finance.

Marina City was also an amalgamation of American and European philosophies, including Alfred North Whitehead's ideas about process and change in human endeavor. Similarly, the antiromantic New Humanism of Irving Babbitt may have led Goldberg to regard the social dimension of architecture as equal to its constructional and formal aspects, though he did not reject the romantic notion of the architect as craftsman. Finally, Vladimir Woytinsky's leftist ideas about bridging aesthetics and politics, crossing social and professional boundaries, and the importance of understanding economics played a role in the Marina City concept.

European and American ideas thus led Goldberg to regard the social and economic dimension of architecture as equal to its formal and constructional aspects. He was very aware of his role as a professional—he saw the architect as social facilitator—in a broad democratic sense. The project's innovative financial strategies, including the manipulation of local and federal urban regulations to obtain housing mortgage insurance, complemented by targeted marketing, came from this sensibility. He effectively used images, models, publications, and exhibitions to create Marina City's public presence: showrooms, brochures, and photos highlighted its heroic scale and abstract form, balancing familiarity with idealism; the careful use of prose in press releases, interviews, and lectures exhorted new forms of urban living. Grounded in economy and commodity exchange, tradition, and innovation, idealism, and pragmatism, Goldberg controlled images of and texts about Marina City to seamlessly migrate between high architecture, building production, and consumer culture.[5]

Marina City's reputation also benefited from Chicago's historical stature. The city was the product of engineering, construction, and infrastructural achievements, and it was the cradle of U.S. architectural developments.[6] In its architectural expression of air, water, rail, car, and pedestrian transportation systems, and by merging European traditions with those of Chicago, Marina City became a Chicago milestone. Although he remained in Mies's shadow in the city, further afield Goldberg, and Marina City's role in the history of twentieth-century architecture, was understood and honored.

Opticalities: Vision, Erasure, Revision

> This presupposes a transformation of the site of architectural production—no longer exclusively located on the construction site, but more and more displaced into the rather immaterial sites of architectural publications, exhibitions and journals. Paradoxically, those are supposedly much more ephemeral media than the building and yet in many ways are much more permanent: they secure a place for an architecture in history, a historical space designed not just by the historians and critics but also by the architects themselves who deployed these media.
> —Beatriz Colomina, *Privacy and Publicity*

Marina City's rise, fall, and rebirth are inseparable not only from the expansion of capitalism, its industrialization of production, and its social and economic contradictions, but also from architectural history and the history of ideas—and their transformation by the emergence of an international economy of images and the dominance of visuality within a consumer society.

In architecture the economy of images—the rule of opticality—took the form, among others, of publications, film, and advertising; in this book we have therefore paid particular attention not only to Goldberg's urban, architectural, engineering, and financial acumen but also his wide-ranging image-building strategies. In seminal books by Le Corbusier, Erich Mendelssohn, Siegfried Giedion, and others, visual representations of modernity dominated architectural consciousness, and Marina City built upon this historical trajectory. Explaining Le Corbusier's approach to windows in modernist architecture, Beatriz Colomina wrote:

> The house is a device to see the world, a mechanism of viewing. Shelter, separation from the outside, is provided by the window's ability to turn the threatening world outside the house into a reassuring picture. The inhabitant is enveloped, wrapped, protected by the pictures.[7]

The view from the Marina City balcony, framed by the apartment's floor-to-ceiling "picture window" typified this—a space defined by Chicago's panorama, or in Colomina's words, "a space that is not made of walls but of images. Images as walls."[8] Marina City's balconies balanced "privacy and publicity," simultaneously opening the apartment to the city and shielding it from noise, showing, in Walter Benjamin's words, that "the living room is a box in the theater of the world."[9] This stage-set quality of Marina City's balconies, and the view that they provided, is best exemplified in the movie sets in which the complex appeared—a form of theatricality that was foreshadowed in Marina City's early showrooms and large wallpaper aerial views that wrapped around them.

Walter Benjamin also theorized twentieth-century buildings as phantasmagoria of light. A modern building was an amalgamation of day and night, light, spectacle, and consumption—as Goldberg called it—"a lighted city."[10] These ideas foreshadowed architecture's involvement with spectacle that later flowered in the architecture and writings of practices such as the Office for Metropolitan Architecture (OMA). Citing images of Coney Island, in *Delirious New York*, Rem Koolhaas observed, "Now, the city itself, is to be lived in shifts; the electric city, phantom offspring of the 'real' city, is an even more powerful instrument for the fulfillment of fantasy."[11]

Yet, unlike the generation of architects that followed, Goldberg remained firmly connected to architecture's material presence, industrial reality, and social ideals, capitalist motivations within humanist democracy.

Nevertheless, many voices remained unheard in Marina City's making. If involved in the project at all, women were mainly interior designers and secretaries, rarely appearing in official photographs unless posing as models. Marina City was born "when affirmative action was white."[12] Goldberg was aware of Chicago's historical tensions between Caucasians and African Americans. Marina City was to be racially integrated from the outset—a fact written in its policies.[13] According to Carl Condit, the first group of occupants included four black tenants; it is not clear whether this continued as more apartments were let. Yet only two persons of color, Tom Young, the West Indian former vice-president of Local 32B, and an unknown woman, appeared in photographs of the groundbreaking; we found only one further person of color in Marina City's archival images—an African American maid in a kitchen.[14]

Marina City's makers worked with the FHA to reclassify single people and families without children as families eligible for federal mortgage benefits. Yet, we found no reference to representation or accommodation of sexual orientation. This is not unexpected given Marina City's historical context—and its client, a white-male-dominated union with strong links to the Catholic Church in a city with a powerful Catholic mayor.

Marina City's main social agenda remained that of upward social mobility for heterosexual, wage-earning middle-class individuals and employment for members of the Janitors' Union. The annual income of all tenants ranged from four-thousand to ninety-thousand dollars, the majority of tenants falling below ten-thousand dollars.[15] More than one hundred Janitors' Union members were employed in the building. This data suggests that Marina City's social goals were primarily economic and that its transformation of class was effected through income and workplace mix—creating jobs for blue-collar workers and consolidating downtown Chicago's urban middle class, side by side with upper-income professionals.

As Marina City's photographs indicate, women, and especially black women, remained in the kitchen or at most adorned Marina City's balconies; black men were altogether invisible. Ideals of labor empowerment and class mobility came, just like modernist ideals including Bauhaus educational principles, in white male clothing.[16]

The history of Marina City to date has—perhaps necessarily—been one of images, with a particularly strong impact in Europe and the Far East. In the process of their dissemination, social narratives were erased, allowing Marina City to stand as a seemingly utopian urban model of formal and structural exuberance, an optical tour de force that sidestepped its dependence on a market-driven economy and specific political and social conditions. The capitalism within its urbanism was erased. This exclusion of economics and politics from many of its writings and visualizations, and from much of the history of architectural modernism in general, removed important tools and presented unrealistic expectations for architects.

Although our work as historians operates in the same world of historical images and texts, opticalities, and erasures, in this book we sought to redress the imbalance. By unpacking and rewrapping the received understanding of Marina City we hope to have presented it not only as a paradigm of enlightened urbanism in its time, but also—if broader conditions permit—as a potential model for a socially, culturally, and economically informed architectural practice.

notes

Introduction (pp. 8–11)

—

Epigraph Reyner Banham, "Walk in the Loop," *Chicago Magazine*, Spring 1965, 27.

1 See Gilbert Cross, "The House the Janitors Built," *Fortune*, November 1962, 152–54, 167; later condensed and reprinted as Gilbert Cross, "The House the Janitors Built," *Readers Digest*, February 1963, 201–204. All references are to the *Fortune* edition.

2 Goldberg's office was involved in some later tenant changes, including the renovations of the 1990s, which dramatically changed the appearance of Marina City's public plaza. The client did not follow much of the architect's recommendations, resulting in the deterioration of the original vision and design for Marina City.

3 Carl Condit described Marina City's development by a labor organization and its relationship to Chicago's urban politics. For critiques of Condit's approach, see Robert Bruegmann, "Myth of the Chicago School," in *Chicago Architecture: Histories, Revisions, Alternatives*, ed. Charles Waldheim and Katerina Rüedi Ray (Chicago: University of Chicago Press, 2005), 15–29; and Carol Willis, "Light, Height, and Site: The Skyscraper in Chicago," in *Chicago Architecture and Design, 1923–1993*, ed. John Zukowsky (Chicago: Art Institute of Chicago, 2000 [1993]), 118–39.

4 Bertrand Goldberg, "Rich is Right," *Inland Architect*, January–February 1982, 6–15; also reprinted in *Goldberg: Dans la Ville / On the City*, ed. Michel Ragon (Paris: Paris Art Center, 1985), 199–208; and Bertrand Goldberg, "The Critical Mass of Urbanism," *Inland Architect*, March–April 1984, 4, 9–12; also reprinted in *Goldberg*, ed. Michel Ragon, 192–97.

Before Marina City (pp. 22–41)

—

Epigraph Betty Blum, *Oral History of Bertrand Goldberg*, (Chicago: Art Institute of Chicago, 1992), 19.

1 Ibid., 3–4. Geoffrey Goldberg, e-mail to the authors, January 13, 2009.

2 Blum, *Oral History of Bertrand Goldberg*, 10.

3 Ibid.

4 When in 1985 Dean Henry N. Cobb gave his Walter Gropius lecture titled "Architecture and the University," he frequently referred to Whitehead's ideas. Henry N. Cobb, *Architecture and the University: Walter Gropius Lecture, April 25, 1985* (Cambridge, MA: Harvard Graduate School of Design, 1986).

5 Blum, *Oral History of Bertrand Goldberg*, 26–27.

6 Ibid., 12.

7 Ibid., 36–37.

8 Ibid., 22.

9 Ibid., 23.

10 Ibid., 24.

11 Ibid.

12 Ibid., 27.

13 Ibid., 25.

14 Ibid., 18–20.

15 Ibid., 19.

16 Ibid., 28.

17 Ibid., 37–38.

18 Ibid., 39.

19 Ibid., 38–39.

20 Bertrand Goldberg, "Acknowledgments of the Artist," in *Goldberg*, ed. Ragon, 6. In his *Oral History*, Goldberg is a little more circumspect, answering a question regarding Mies with: "a surrogate father? Perhaps." Blum, *Oral History of Bertrand Goldberg*, 99.

21 Blum, *Oral History of Bertrand Goldberg*, 43.

22 Ibid., 41.

23 Ibid., 44.

24 Ibid., 152.

25 Ibid., 46–49.

26 Ibid., 88–89.

27 Bertrand Goldberg, "Marina City, Chicago, Illinois," September 1965, 8. Bertrand Goldberg Collection, Ryerson and Burnham Archives, The Art Institute of Chicago.

28 Johnson was an acquaintance of Goldberg's Bauhaus roommate Michael van Beuren. Blum, *Oral History of Bertrand Goldberg*, 54; Fred Keck also employed architects Ralph Rapson and Stanley Tigerman. Robert Boyce mentions that Goldberg was a "frequent visitor" to Keck's office in the 1930s and was tutored by Fred Keck himself. See Robert Boyce, *Keck and Keck* (New York: Princeton Architectural Press, 1993), 11.

29 Fisher's prefabricated houses are mentioned in Alison Arief and Bryan Burkhart, *Pre-Fab* (Layton: Gibbs Smith Publisher, 2002), 15–16. See also Burnham Kelly, *The Prefabrication of Houses* (New York: Wiley & Sons / The Technology Press of MIT, 1951).

30 Howard T. Fisher's biographical sketch, Harvard University, http://www.gis. dce.harvard.edu/fisher/HTFisher.htm, accessed January 2, 2009.

31 Blum, *Oral History of Bertrand Goldberg*, 113–14.

32 Ibid., 67.

33 Ibid., 71.

34 Interview with Geoffrey Goldberg, undated.

35 See Bertrand Goldberg, "Kindergarten Plauderei" (Kindergarten chats), *Inland Architect* 30, no. 2 (March/April 1986): 26–29.

36 See *PLUS: Orientations of Contemporary Architecture*, supplement to *Architectural Forum*, December 1938.

37 Blum, *Oral History of Bertrand Goldberg*, 75–77; and Ragon, *Goldberg*, 168.

38 Ragon, *Goldberg*, 168.

39 The building's cost is mentioned in Bertrand Goldberg Archive, "Higginson House," G. Goldberg + Associates, http://www.bertrandgoldberg.org/ works/higginson_house.html, accessed December 27, 2008; The solar heating system is mentioned in Ragon, *Goldberg*, 15.

40 Blum, *Oral History of Bertrand Goldberg*, 126.

41 Ibid., 102.

42 Ibid., 103.

43 Ibid.

44 Press release, Bertrand Goldberg and Associates, February 29, 1960, 2. Bertrand Goldberg Collection, Ryerson and Burnham Archives, The Art Institute of Chicago; Blum, *Oral History of Bertrand Goldberg*, 109–110.

45 Blum, *Oral History of Bertrand Goldberg*, 110.

46 Ibid., 111.

47 Ibid., 112.

48 Ibid.

49 One of the Unican bathrooms is in the permanent collection of the Walker Art Center in Minneapolis, Minnesota, another is at the Art Institute of Chicago, and Frank Lloyd Wright purchased two more. Press Release, Bertrand Goldberg and Associates, February 29, 1960, 2. Bertrand Goldberg Collection, Ryerson and Burnham Archives, The Art Institute of Chicago.

50 Blum, *Oral History of Bertrand Goldberg*, 112.

51 The date of incorporation was October 22, 1954; the office was formed to carry out, among others, "the construction of streets, bridges, parks, houses, apartments…" E-mail from Geoffrey Goldberg to the authors, March 10, 2009.

52 Little is known about Claire Uehlein, an intellectual from Chicago's Hyde Park and Goldberg's first wife. They married in the mid-1940s, but Claire died shortly thereafter. Interview with Geoffrey Goldberg, December 12, 2008. See also Black Mountain College Project, Goldberg Art Memorial Workshop Building, at http://

www.bmcproject.org, accessed June 13, 2009. This gives the date of her death as November 25, 1945.

53 Richard Buckminster Fuller, *Your Private Sky, Richard Buckminster Fuller, The Art of Design Science*, eds. Joachim Krause and Claude Lichtenstein (Baden, Switzerland: Lars Müller; Zürich: Museum für Gestaltung, 1999), 316.

54 For I. M. Pei's Apartment helix project, see Klaus Herdeg, *The Decorated Diagram: Harvard Architecture and the Failure of the Bauhaus Legacy* (Cambridge, MA: MIT Press, 1983), 17.

55 Blum, *Oral History of Bertrand Goldberg*, 165.

56 Ibid., 141.

57 Ragon, *Goldberg*, 74.

58 Blum, *Oral History of Bertrand Goldberg*, 141–42.

59 Ragon, *Goldberg*, 63.

60 Helstein taught the history of labor at Roosevelt College (now Roosevelt University) in Chicago. Interview with Geoffrey Goldberg and the authors, December 20, 2007.

Unpacking Marina City (pp. 42–69)

—

Epigraph Blum, *Oral History of Bertrand Goldberg*, 185.

1 Ibid., 160.

2 About McFetridge's AFL-CIO affiliation see T. Smart, "Marina City Gets Bad News—Taxes Going Up," *Chicago's American*, May 14, 1964, Bertrand Goldberg Collection, Ryerson and Burnham Archives, The Art Institute of Chicago; Blum, *Oral History of Bertrand Goldberg*, 155.

3 Eric Arnesen, *Encyclopedia of U.S. Labor and Working-Class History* (London: Routledge, 2006), 1227.

4 Adam Cohen and Elizabeth Taylor, *American Pharaoh: Mayor Richard J. Daley—His Battle for Chicago and the Nation* (Boston: Back Bay, 2001).

5 "Profile: William L. McFetridge," press release, February 29, 1960, Bertrand Goldberg Associates, Bertrand Goldberg Collection, Ryerson and Burnham Archives, The Art Institute of Chicago.

6 "Union Sells Interest in Marina City," *Chicago Daily News*, July 11, 1964.

7 "Progress Report; 'On the Way Up' In Marina City," *Chicago Daily News*, April 9, 1962.

8 "Profile: Charles Swibel," press release, undated, Bertrand Goldberg Associates, 1, Bertrand Goldberg Collection, Ryerson and Burnham Archives, The Art Institute of Chicago.

9 Ibid.

10 Ibid.

11 Cohen and Taylor, *American Pharaoh*, 199.

12 "From a Ghetto to Marina Tower—The Epic Of Charles Swibel," *Chicago Sun-Times*, July 25, 1965, 8, 58–59.

13 Blum, *Oral History of Bertrand Goldberg*, 75.

14 "Profile: Charles Swibel," 1.

15 "Progress Report; 'On the Way Up' In Marina City."

16 "From a Ghetto," 58–59.

17 Ibid.

18 "Profile: Charles Swibel," 2; and "How Project Got Its Name," *Chicago Daily News*, February 1, 1962.

19 Smart, "Marina City Gets Bad News."

20 From the suggested statement for Bertrand Goldberg for Marina City's groundbreaking ceremony, undated. Goldberg Family Archives.

21 Gerald D. Schein, "Labor Sponsors," *Real Estate Forum*, February 1963, 118.

22 Ibid., 119.

23 Press release, Bertrand Goldberg and Associates, February 29, 1960, 3, Bertrand Goldberg Collection, Ryerson and Burnham Archives, The Art Institute of Chicago.

24 "Convenience of High-Rise Living" from *Marina City, A City Within a City*, undated and unpaginated brochure, Bertrand Goldberg Collection, Ryerson and Burnham Archives, The Art Institute of Chicago.

25 Although the *New York Times* obituary stated Severud's name as Fred, Bertold Weinberg assured us in repeated conversations that his name was Ferd, short for Ferdinand. Katerina Rüedi Ray, three telephone conversations with and two sets of written comments from Bertold Weinberg, June 2009.

26 "A City within a City" was the title of many essays, lectures, and marketing brochures by Goldberg.

27 For a full listing see *Marina City: A City Within a City*, the Marina City Management Corporation, undated, Bertrand Goldberg Collection, Ryerson and Burnham Archives, The Art Institute of Chicago.

28 Press release, "Plans for Marina City, Chicago's First Downtown Housing Project, Are Revealed," Bertrand Goldberg and Associates, undated, 3, Bertrand Goldberg Collection, Ryerson and Burnham Archives, The Art Institute of Chicago.

29 R. Gray, "Central Core Soars to 24 Stories—36 more to Go," *Chicago Daily News*, (August 5, 1961), Bertrand Goldberg Collection, Ryerson and Burnham Archives, The Art Institute of Chicago.

30 "Chicago's Brightest Architect on Men, Buildings, the Future"; R. Moore, quoting Bertrand Goldberg, *Chicago Sun Times*, March 1, 1960.

31 Marina City Fact Sheet, Marina City Management Corporation, April 1964, Bertrand Goldberg Collection, Ryerson and Burnham Archives, The Art Institute of Chicago.

32 Image caption for a photograph of a two-bedroom Marina City model apartment, Bertrand Goldberg Collection, Ryerson and Burnham Archives, The Art Institute of Chicago.

33 Image caption, Marina City one-bedroom model apartment, Bertrand Goldberg Collection, Ryerson and Burnham Archives, The Art Institute of Chicago.

34 J. Gavin, "First Car Spirals Into Marina City Garage," *Chicago Tribune*, February 15, 1963, Bertrand Goldberg Collection, Ryerson and Burnham Archives, The Art Institute of Chicago.

35 Pauline Saliga, "To Build a Better Mousetrap: Design in Chicago, 1920–1970," in *Chicago Architecture and Design, 1923-1993*, ed. John Zukowsky (Chicago: The Art Institute of Chicago, 2000), 278–79.

36 "National Design Center: Chicago Version," *Inland Architect*, November 1964, 19.

37 Pauline Saliga, *Oral History of George Danforth* (Chicago: Art Institute of Chicago, 2003), 74–76.

38 Bertrand Goldberg, "Marina City Lecture" (Parts One and Two), presented at a seminar on the Architectural Aspects of the Edmonton Civic Plan, September 27, 1962. Bertrand Goldberg Archive, http://www.bertrandgoldberg.org/resources/marina_city2.html, accessed March 11, 2009.

39 See Cross, "The House the Janitors Built," 152–54, 167.

40 *Marina City Newsletter* 2, no. 2 (July 1965).

The Structure (pp. 70–91)

—

Epigraph Carl W. Condit, *The Chicago School of Architecture: A History of Commercial and Public Buildings in the Chicago Area, 1875–1925*, (Chicago: University of Chicago Press, 1964), 219.

1 Geoffrey Goldberg, *Goldberg*, self-published, 185.

2 Interview with Geoffrey Goldberg and the authors, Chicago, February 1, 2008.

3 We have been unable to ascertain Ms. Bouchelle's first name.

4 Bertold Weinberg, telephone conversation with Katerina Rüedi Ray, June 5, 2009.

5 Blum, *Oral History of Bertrand Goldberg*, 167.

6 Bertold Weinberg, telephone conversation with Katerina Rüedi Ray, June 5, 2009.

7 "Consultants on Marina City", Bertrand Goldberg Associates document, September 26, 1960, David Sullivan Collection, Box 81, Folder 4, Archives of Labor and Urban Affairs, Wayne State University.

8 "Two Tall, Lean Towers of Chicago Really Don't Lean at All," *Chicago Sunday Tribune*, May 13, 1961.

9 "Concrete Makes Architectural History in Chicago," *Plasterer and Cement Mason*, March 1963, cover.

10 Schein, "Labor Sponsors," 123.

11 *Marina City, A City Within a City*, undated and unpaginated brochure, Bertrand Goldberg Collection, Ryerson and Burnham Archives, The Art Institute of Chicago.

12 "Chicago Leaders Celebrate First Anniversary of Huge Marina City Development, 588 Foot High Core of First Apartment Tower Complete," press release, author unknown, November 22, 1961, Bertrand Goldberg Collection, Ryerson and Burnham Archives, The Art Institute of Chicago.

13 Carl W. Condit, "The Structural System of Adler and Sullivan's Garrick Theater Building," *Technology and Culture* 5, no. 4 (Autumn, 1964): 531. This was disputed, however, by Bert Weinberg in a telephone conversation with Katerina Rüedi Ray, June 5, 2009.

14 Most cranes operating from the ground at the time could only reach a height of fourteen stories.

15 McFetridge, report to the Janitors' Union's executive board, June 12, 1962, 2, David Sullivan Collection, Box 80, Folder 25, Archives of Labor and Urban Affairs, Wayne State University.

16 "Cranes to Help Move Tenants into Marina," *Chicago Daily Tribune*, October 5, 1962.

17 Bertold Weinberg, "3. Marina City—Towers," *Civil Engineering*, December 1962.

18 Bertold Weinberg, interview with Geoffrey Goldberg, December 17, 2005.

19 Letter, William McFetridge to David Sullivan, November 3, 1961, David Sullivan Collection, Box 80, Folder 23, Archives of Labor and Urban Affairs, Wayne State University.

20 Gray, "Central Core Soars to 24 Stories—36 more to Go."

21 "Towers in Race At Marina City," *Chicago's American*, March 23, 1962.

22 Mullions were spaced two feet one-half inch on center, permitting desk arrangements along the exterior wall on a modular basis and maintaining a sense of transparency.

23 "World's First All Lead Building," *Lead: Lead Industries Association* 31, no. 3, 1967.

24 The article also notes that installation was carried out by the Allied Lead Construction Company of Chicago, subcontracted to Eric A. Borg Company, also of Chicago. Ibid.

25 Carl W. Condit, *Chicago, 1930–1970: Building, Planning, and Urban Technology* (Chicago: The University of Chicago Press, 1974), 73.

26 T. Buck, "The Secret of Marina City 'Tree Houses,' Giants Changing the Skyline of the City," *Chicago Tribune*, September 10, 1961.

27 Bertold Weinberg, conversation with Katerina Rüedi Ray, June 5, 2009.

28 "Electrical Supply to Marina City," AIEE Great Lakes District Meeting, April 25–27, 1962, 1–2, Bertrand Goldberg Collection, Ryerson and Burnham Archives, The Art Institute of Chicago.

29 Ibid.

30 Buck, "The Secret of Marina City 'Tree Houses.'"

31 "Chicago's Brightest Architect on Men, Buildings, The Future," unknown source, probably December 1960, Bertrand Goldberg Collection, Ryerson and Burnham Archives, The Art Institute of Chicago.

32 Bertrand Goldberg, "Space Savings at Marina City," Bertrand Goldberg Collection, Ryerson and Burnham Archives, The Art Institute of Chicago.

33 Ibid.

34 Ibid.

35 "How They Keep the Ice from Damaging the Boats," *News*, February 4, 1965.

36 Although McHugh Construction claimed to have come up with the idea of the fiberglass molds, Goldberg's experience with fiberglass for the Florsheim kitchen may also have influenced the office to test the idea.

37 "Here is something new about the weather," *Chicago Tribune*, February 13, 1965.

38 Smart, "Marina City Gets Bad News"; "Settlements in Marina City Deaths Told," *Chicago Tribune*, October 6, 1966; and Bertold Weinberg, conversation with Katerina Rüedi Ray, June 5, 2009.

39 "Safety Devices Hailed as Saving 6 in Marina Fall," *Chicago Evening American*, June 20, 1962.

The Deal (pp. 92–105)

—

Epigraph Barr Ferree, "Economic Conditions of Architecture in America," *Proceedings of the Twenty-Seventh Annual Convention of the American Institute of Architects* (Chicago 1893), 228–41.

1 Condit, *Chicago: 1930–1970*, 118.

2 Letter, Bertrand Goldberg to James Smith, Chief Underwriter, FHA, Merchandise Mart, Chicago, August 13, 1959, and letter to William McFetridge, probably from Lester Asher, attorney for the Janitors' Union, September 9, 1959, David Sullivan Collection, Box 80, Folder 18, Archives of Labor and Urban Affairs, Wayne State University.

3 Press release, author unknown, possibly Goldberg, September 17, 1959, 3, Bertrand Goldberg Collection, Ryerson and Burnham Archives, The Art Institute of Chicago.

4 "Once in a Century," prospectus for the Marina City site, undated, 1, Bertrand Goldberg Collection, Ryerson and Burnham Archives, The Art Institute of Chicago, see also 1959 *Housing Market Analysis Report* of the Chicago Area Central Committee, available at: http://www.uic.edu/depts/lib/specialcoll/services/rjd/findingaids/ChicagoCentralf.html, accessed March 9, 2009.

5 "Plans for Marina City, Chicago's First Downtown Housing Project, Are Revealed," Bertrand Goldberg Associates, press release, undated, 4, Bertrand Goldberg Collection, Ryerson and Burnham Archives, The Art Institute of Chicago.

6 "Once in A Century," 2.

7 "Chicago's Brightest Architect on Men, Buildings, The Future."

8 "Plans for Marina City, Chicago's First Downtown Housing Project, Are Revealed," press release, Bertrand Goldberg Associates, February 29, 1960, 3, Bertrand Goldberg Collection, Ryerson and Burnham Archives, The Art Institute of Chicago.

9 Press release, author unknown, possibly Goldberg, September 17, 1959, 2, Bertrand Goldberg Collection, Ryerson and Burnham Archives, The Art Institute of Chicago.

10 William McFetridge, cited in Cross, "The House the Janitors Built," 154.

11 Blum, *Oral History of Bertrand Goldberg*, 167.

12 "Chicago's Brightest Architect."

13 Blum, *Oral History of Bertrand Goldberg*, 160.

14 J. Ullman, "C&NW Offers Riverfront Plot," *Chicago Sun-Times*, December 1, 1959.

15 "Once in a Century," 6.

16 BSEIU, *Report to Locals*, 30 September 1959, 1, David Sullivan Collection, Box 80, Folder 18, Archives of Labor and Urban Affairs, Wayne State University.

17 *A Need for Valor*, draft, Service Employees International Union Historical Collection, box 4, folders 3–4 titled, *A Need for Valor* (original manuscript), 1–274 with cover letter, 1983, Archives of Labor and Urban Affairs, Wayne State University.

18 Press release, undated, author unknown, Bertrand Goldberg Collection, Ryerson and Burnham Archives, The Art Institute of Chicago.

19 Ullman, "C&NW Offers Riverfront Plot."

20 Cross, "The House the Janitors Built," 153.

21 The north section, planned for offices, shops and other businesses sat on land assessed at $3.50 per square foot totaling $19,525 in taxes; in the south section the residential towers sat on land assessed at $10 per square foot, totaling $128,342 in taxes. Smart, "Marina City Gets Bad News."

22 Ibid.

23 Interview with Geoffrey Goldberg, undated.

24 "Plans for Marina City, Chicago's First Downtown Housing Project, Are Revealed," press release, BGA, 29 February 1960, last page (attached as a separate statement by John L. Waner), Bertrand Goldberg Collection, Ryerson and Burnham Archives, The Art Institute of Chicago.

25 The National Housing Act of 1934 created the Federal Housing Administration and, under Title II of the Act, established mortgage insurance programs of which Section 207 related to insurance for multifamily projects, http://www.hud.gov/offices/adm/about/admguide/history.cfm, accessed January 6, 2008.

26 Letter, carbon copy, unclear authorship, most likely from BSEIU attorney Lester Asher to McFetridge, September 9, 1959, 1, David Sullivan Collection, Box 80, Folder 18, Archives of Labor and Urban Affairs, Wayne State University.

27 The mortgage term was for thirty-nine years at a maximum interest rate of 5.25 percent, Issued under Section 207 of Title II of the 1934 National Housing Act, it represented only 80 percent of the costs of the residential component of Marina City—the remainder was covered by the Janitors' Union partners and the banks providing the construction loans. "From Bertrand Goldberg Associates, For Immediate Release," July 7, 1960, Bertrand Goldberg Collection, Ryerson and Burnham Archives, The Art Institute of Chicago.

28 Ibid.

29 "Ground Broken for Marina City," *Chicago Sun-Times*, November 23, 1960; "Kinzie Cabin on Spot First," *Chicago's American*, November 22, 1960.

30 M. Stevens, "First Use of Section 207 of Federal Housing Act for Downtown Apartments Announced by Commissioner Zimmerman of FHA," press release, June 23, 1960; "Profile: William L. McFetridge."

31 Blum, *Oral History of Bertrand Goldberg*, 161.

32 The Janitors' Union and Local No. 1 were both "McFetridge's organizations"; Local 32B was David Sullivan's local union; the Pension Trust (West Coast) treasurer, Jay Raskin, like Sullivan, would later become a chief detractor of the project. "Ground Broken for Marina City." According to Bertold Weinberg, shortly before the commissioning of Marina City, new federal legislation had permitted unions to invest their pension funds in mortgage securities but we have not been able to locate more information. Bertold Weinberg, telephone conversation with Katerina Rüedi Ray, June 13, 2009.

33 Cross, "The House the Janitors Built," 153.

34 "Marina City," *Chicago Daily News*, July 17, 1960, confirmed formal approval of $18 million from the FHA, an unstated amount of private capital, and $10.6 million from the Janitors' Union; Cross, "The House the Janitors Built," 154.

35 Letter, Bertrand Goldberg to James Smith, chief underwriter, FHA, Merchandise Mart, Chicago, August 13, 1959, David Sullivan Collection, Box 80, Folder 18, Archives of Labor and Urban Affairs, Wayne State University; "Marina City," *Chicago Daily News*, July 17, 1960.

36 "Kinzie Cabin on Spot First," *Chicago's American*, November 22, 1960.

37 "For Immediate Release," Merrill Schwartz, public relations, November 15, 1960, Bertrand Goldberg Collection, Ryerson and Burnham Archives, The Art Institute of Chicago.

38 Cross, "The House the Janitors Built," 154.

39 "3 Marina City Interests Sold," *Chicago Sun-Times*, July 11, 1964.

40 The Consortium included seventeen other partners: the Bronx, Brooklyn, Buffalo, East Brooklyn, Eastchester, Erie County, Greenwich, Hamburg, Kings County, Mechanics Exchange, Queens County, Ridgewood, and Rochester savings banks, as well as the Roosevelt Savings Bank of the City of New York, and the savings banks of Utica, Union Square, and Watertown. "$5 million Continental Bank Loan Completes Marina City Financing," press release, Marina City Development Corporation, undated, Bertrand Goldberg Collection, Ryerson and Burnham Archives, The Art Institute of Chicago. For Goldberg's and Swibel's role as publicists see Cross, "The House the Janitors Built," 154.

41 "The Continental Illinois came through again, notifying Swibel it would lend an additional $5 million...Meanwhile McFetridge had pledged $12 million of the union's assets to guarantee that the project would be completed." Cross, "The House the Janitors Built," 154.

42 Cross, "The House the Janitors Built," 154. The article did not specify who these lenders were.

43 Ibid.

44 "Interim Report, Marina City Project," (c. 1960), 5. David Sullivan Collection, Box 80, Folder 20, Archives of Labor and Urban Affairs, Wayne State University.

45 The lessee was the newly formed Marina City Garage and Parking Corporation. The lease guaranteed a minimum rental return of five million dollars to the Marina City Building Corporation over twenty-five years.

46 J. Gavin, "Marina City Financing Completed," *Chicago Tribune*, September 1961.

47 Draft loan, July 28, 1961, North Marina City Building Corporation and Continental Illinois National Bank and Trust Company, David Sullivan Collection, Box 80, Folder 23, Archives of Labor and Urban Affairs, Wayne State University.

48 J. Haas, "'For Rent' Sign Unnecessary Here," *Chicago Daily News*, December 11, 1961; J. Gavin, "First Car Spirals Into Marina City Garage," *Chicago Tribune*, February 15, 1963.

49 Applicants' credit ratings were checked, and applicants were rated along with their levels of interest in the facilities in the complex, including their intent to join the Marina City Yacht Club. "Marina City Cuts 1,500 Applicants, More to Go," *Chicago's American*, April 18, 1962.

50 "Ground Broken for Marina City."

51 Press Release, BGA, February 15, 1960, 1, Bertrand Goldberg Collection, Ryerson and Burnham Archives, The Art Institute of Chicago.

52 Blum, *Oral History of Bertrand Goldberg*, 187.

53 "Design for Business," from *Marina City: Design for Business,* a marketing brochure by the Marina Management Corporation; undated and unpaginated brochure, Bertrand Goldberg Collection, Ryerson and Burnham Archives, The Art Institute of Chicago.

54 "Marina Gets Design Center," *Chicago Sun-Times*, September 28, 1962.

55 "Earnings '64: New Highs...New Records," *Illinois Banker*, February 26, 1965, 6, 23.

56 "This Deal Smells," *Chicago Tribune*, February 11, 1965.

57 E. Gilbreth, "World of Marina City, Lowdown on the High Life," *Chicago Daily News*, May 6, 1967.

58 Unsigned minutes (if signed the minutes would have to have been handed over to FHA eventually), Special Meeting of Shareholders of the Marina City Building Corporation and the North Marina City Building Corporation, December 17, 1963, David Sullivan Collection, Box 80, Folder 29, Archives of Labor and Urban Affairs, Wayne State University.

59 U.S. Census Bureau, "Historical Income Tables–Families," http://www.census.gov/hhes/www/income/histinc/f07ar.html, accessed March 12, 2009.

60 Gilbreth, "World of Marina City." The rentals were reported to be "beyond the reach of all but the best paid wage earners," Cross, "The House the Janitors Built," 167.

61 Blum, *Oral History of Bertrand Goldberg*, 183.

62 "Fight Against Recession Launched at Marina City, Flow of First Twenty Million Dollars Begins at Marina City," press release, Bertrand Goldberg Associates, February 16, 1961, Bertrand Goldberg Collection, Ryerson and Burnham Archives, The Art Institute of Chicago.

63 Ibid.

64 "Heart of City Turning Into A Boom Town," *Chicago Sun-Times*, March 20, 1961.

65 "Chicago Leaders Celebrate First Anniversary of Huge Marina City Development, 588 Foot High Core of First Apartment Tower Complete," press release, author unknown, November 22, 1961, Bertrand Goldberg Collection, Ryerson and Burnham Archives, The Art Institute of Chicago; Schein, "Labor Sponsors."

66 Anonymous, initials AR, "The Union and Marina City," *Buildings*, February 3, 1961, David Sullivan Collection, Box 80, Folder 21, Archives of Labor and Urban Affairs, Wayne State University.

67 "Chicagoans Buy Marina City," *Chicago's American*, July 11, 1964, Section 1.

68 Notes re Marina City (handwritten note states per AB, likely to be Aaron Benenson) June 9, 1961, David Sullivan Collection, Box 80, Folder 22, Archives of Labor and Urban Affairs, Wayne State University.

69 Memo, Aaron Benenson, Lester Asher to David Sullivan, October 4, 1962, David Sullivan Collection, Box 80, Folder 26, Archives of Labor and Urban Affairs, Wayne State University.

70 Memo, William Goodstein to William McFetridge, February 28, 1963, David Sullivan Collection, Box 80, Folder 27, Archives of Labor and Urban Affairs, Wayne State University.

71 Cross, "The House the Janitors Built," 167.

72 "Chicagoans Buy Marina City," Section 1.

73 Letter, David Sullivan to William McFetridge, May 22, 1963, David Sullivan Collection, Box 80, Folder 27, Archives of Labor and Urban Affairs, Wayne State University.

74 "Intra-union squabble over Marina City leads to sellout by three sponsors," Labor Briefs section, *Business Week*, July 18, 1964, 106.

75 "Union Sells Interest in Marina City," *Chicago Daily News*, July 11, 1964.

76 Response from D. W. Martin, of the United Housing Foundation, June 22, 1962, David Sullivan Collection, Box 80, Folder 25, Archives of Labor and Urban Affairs, Wayne State University. Abraham E. Kazan, president of the same organization, was also reported to be highly critical of the project. Cross, "The House the Janitors Built," 167.

77 "Building Service Union Sells Marina City Control: Swibel Pays $2.6 Millions, Assumes Lien," *Chicago Tribune*, Sunday, July 12, 1964, Section 4, 1.

78 "3 Marina City Interests Sold," *Chicago Sun-Times*, July 11, 1964.

79 "Kup's Column: Now Hear This: Bill McFetridge," *Chicago Sun-Times*, May 19, 1964.

80 "Chicagoans Buy Marina City," Section 1.

81 Blum, *Oral History of Bertrand Goldberg*, 173.

82 The article went on to criticize not only Swibel but also Daley: "When Mayor Daley appointed Swibel to the CHA in 1956, the mayor said that Swibel was reported to be 'one of the most energetic, attentive workers on the Committee for the Rehabilitation of Man.' Informally known as the Skid Row Committee, it still numbers Swibel among its members." "Bias in CHA Exec's Hotels–White Only Rule," *Chicago Courier*, November 17, 1963.

83 *Chicago's American* reported that the entire management team of Marks and Company had left the firm to set up Randolph Realty Company, at the same address and with the same officers holding similar positions at the new company. Swibel was apparently not associated with this office, but had an office there. "Swibel Quits Realty Firm, New One Set Up," *Chicago's American*, May 5 1966; "$2-Million Suit Accuses Swibel," *Chicago Sun-Times*, June 16, 1966; "Swibel Named in $2 Million Fraud Action," *Chicago's American*, June 16, 1966, 1–4; "CHA Chief, 5 Others Looted Trust, Suit Says," *Chicago Daily News*, June 16, 1966.

84 Swibel was eventually "pushed" out of the CHA in 1985, under allegations of patronage and mismanagement. Nathaniel Sheppard Jr., "Chicago Housing Chief Under Fire, Quits as Agency is Reorganized," *New York Times*, July 9, 1982; Tom Beading, Pat Cooper, Grace Palladino, and Peter Pieragostini, *A Need for Valor, The Roots of the Service Employees International Union 1902–1992* (Washington DC: Service Employees International Union), 22–27.

85 Memo, Lester Asher to David Sullivan, February 2, 1967, David Sullivan Collection, Box 81, Folder 23, Archives of Labor and Urban Affairs, Wayne State University.

86 Letter, William Goodstein to Aaron Benenson, February 10, 1967, David Sullivan Collection, Box 81, Folder 23, Archives of Labor and Urban Affairs, Wayne State University.

87 "L. J. Sheridan to manage Marina Office Building," *Realty and Building*, April 29, 1967, attached to letter, William Goodstein to Aaron Benenson, February 10, 1967, David Sullivan Collection, Box 81, Folder 23, Archives of Labor and Urban Affairs, Wayne State University.

88 Cohen and Taylor, *American Pharaoh*, 294. Also, when Marina City apartments were turned into condominiums, valuable contents of the complex, such as the Vasarely paintings in the theater lobby, were auctioned off.

89 Geoffrey Goldberg, email to the authors, October 13, 2008.

90 In May 1964 it was announced that real estate taxes on the twin towers were to be increased substantially, based on a significant revaluing of the land by the City of Chicago. Smart, "Marina City Gets Bad News."

91 "Marina City president confirms plans to offer condominiums in fall," *Chicago Daily News*, August 5, 1977. When ownership passed to Texas-based Marina City Associates, and the mortgage to the Continental Savings Association of Houston, the complex became yet another element of a real estate portfolio and was neglected by its long-distance owners until they themselves failed and the commercial spaces ended up in bankruptcy court.

92 The Janitors' Union was unwilling to underwrite the project financially during the economic downturn of 1961 or be patient with gaining long-term control.

The Image (pp. 106–131)
—

Epigraph Kup's Column, *Chicago Sun-Times*, October 5, 1966.

1 Press Release, Bertrand Goldberg and Associates, February 29, 1960, Bertrand Goldberg Collection, Ryerson and

Burnham Archives, The Art Institute of Chicago.

[2] The imaging of Marina City occurred in the context of the imaging of modernist buildings like Mies's Barcelona Pavilion in which photography played an equal role to actual built form in its status as an icon of twentieth-century architecture.

[3] Cross, "The House the Janitors Built," 154.

[4] One of Goldberg's book projects was a 1952 oversize portfolio called *Freight*—an elegant publication of poems by John Frederick Nims and drawings by Richard Florsheim. It was encased in fiberglass covers measuring two by three feet. Goldberg also produced elaborate printed publications for projects such as Unicel and Unishelter.

[5] This rough study model showing Marina City as three towers was most likely made of chipboard or other similar type of paper, as documented in a small black and white photograph, located in the Bertrand Goldberg Collection, Ryerson and Burnham Archives, The Art Institute of Chicago.

[6] The inscription on the back of the model photographs gives the date of August 1961 and the location as the Continental Illinois Building, Bertrand Goldberg Collection, Ryerson and Burnham Archives, The Art Institute of Chicago.

[7] Blum, *Oral History of Bertrand Goldberg*, 162.

[8] "Marina City Ground Breaking," event program, November 22, 1960, Bertrand Goldberg Collection, Ryerson and Burnham Archives, The Art Institute of Chicago.

[9] "Marina City: 1810–1960" in *Marina City: A New Dimension in Urban Living,* Marina City Groundbreaking Ceremony Brochure, November 22, 1960, Bertrand Goldberg Collection, Ryerson and Burnham Archives, The Art Institute of Chicago.

[10] William McFetridge, "A Message to Chicago" in *Marina City: A New Dimension in Urban Living,* Marina City Groundbreaking Ceremony Brochure, November 22, 1960, Bertrand Goldberg Collection, Ryerson and Burnham Archives, The Art Institute of Chicago.

[11] "Focal Point of Urban Living," in *Marina City: Design for Business*, a marketing brochure by the Marina Management Corporation; undated and unpaginated brochure, Bertrand Goldberg Collection, Ryerson and Burnham Archives, The Art Institute of Chicago.

[12] McFetridge, the Chicago Parks District's vice-president, was on the Chicago Planetarium Society's board as part of a new shared governance structure between the two institutions recommended by a committee, convened by Richard J. Daley, to advance astronomical knowledge and bolster the space race's visibility.

[13] *Celestial Map* for November 22, 1960, presented on November 22, 1961. The caption stated: "This building began on the 22nd of day of November 1960 A.D. according to the Gregorian calendar. The planets in the heavens were as shown on this celestial map. The universal language of astronomy will permit men forever to understand and know this date. Marina City and its towers were the dream of William L. McFetridge, the planning of Charles R. Swibel, and the architecture of Bertrand Goldberg." Bertrand Goldberg Collection, Ryerson and Burnham Archives, The Art Institute of Chicago.

[14] Bertrand Goldberg Associates Press Release, January 5, 1962, Bertrand Goldberg Collection, Ryerson and Burnham Archives, The Art Institute of Chicago; See reference to model apartments in Com Ed advertisement, *Inland Architect*, January 1963, 3.

[15] Bertrand Goldberg, press release, January 9, 1962, Bertrand Goldberg Collection, Ryerson and Burnham Archives, The Art Institute of Chicago.

[16] Goldberg explained the perception of spaciousness not only as an issue of the plan's openness, but also a consequence of the nonrectilinear space that he felt changed the experience of acoustic, lighting, and temperature conditions. Blum, *Oral History of Bertrand Goldberg*, 157.

[17] Cross, "The House the Janitors Built," 154, 167.

[18] A. T. Burch, "Marina Towers: One of Chicago's Living Art Forms," *Chicago Daily News*, September 5, 1964.

[19] Marina City Fact Sheet, Marina Management Corporation, April 1964, 2, Bertrand Goldberg Collection, Ryerson and Burnham Archives, The Art Institute of Chicago.

[20] Later in his career Goldberg established within Bertrand Goldberg Associates a separate company (Copy Corp) to print all the BGA documents, books, drawings, etc., in house. Notes from Geoffrey Goldberg, February 2009.

[21] "Design for Business" in *Marina City: Design for Business,* Bertrand Goldberg Collection, Ryerson and Burnham Archives, The Art Institute of Chicago.

[22] Interestingly, both followed the "square book" format of key Bauhaus books such as the Bauhaus 1923 exhibition catalog.

[23] For images of the Lakeshore Drive Apartments marketing brochure see David Dunster, *Chicago Architecture*, 99.

[24] *Marina City: A City within a City,* produced by the Marina City Management Corporation, undated (probably early 1960s), Bertrand Goldberg Collection, Ryerson and Burnham Archives, The Art Institute of Chicago.

[25] "Core Concept of High Rise Living" in *Marina City: A City within a City,* produced by the Marina City Management Corporation, undated (probably early 1960s), Bertrand Goldberg Collection, Ryerson and Burnham Archives, The Art Institute of Chicago.

[26] Bertrand Goldberg Collection, Ryerson and Burnham Archives, The Art Institute of Chicago.

[27] "View from the Heights" in *Marina City: A City within a City*, produced by the Marina City Management Corporation, undated, Bertrand Goldberg Collection, Ryerson and Burnham Archives, The Art Institute of Chicago.

[28] "All Electric Living," in *Marina City: A City within a City*, produced by the Marina City Management Corporation, undated, Bertrand Goldberg Collection, Ryerson and Burnham Archives, The Art Institute of Chicago.

[29] Business brochure, *Marina City: Design for Business*, Bertrand Goldberg Collection, Ryerson and Burnham Archives, The Art Institute of Chicago.

[30] "Office Planning Aid," in *Marina City: Design for Business*, Bertrand Goldberg Collection, Ryerson and Burnham Archives, The Art Institute of Chicago.

[31] "Convenience of High-Rise Living," in *Marina City: Design for Business*, Bertrand Goldberg Collection, Ryerson and Burnham Archives, The Art Institute of Chicago.

[32] For a thorough discussion about the Hedrich-Blessing firm, see Robert Sobieszek, "The Architectural Photography of Hedrich-Blessing," in *Chicago Architecture*, 181–95; and Robert A. Sobieszek, ed., *The Architectural Photography of Hedrich-Blessing* (New York: Holt, Rinehart and Winston, 1984).

[33] See Sobieszek, "The Architectural Photography of Hedrich-Blessing," in *Chicago Architecture*, 186, 189.

[34] Ibid., 186, 190.

[35] Goldberg's photographs from European travels in the 1950s show visual sophistication beyond conventional architectural training; he had studied with the renowned photographer Aaron Siskind at the Institute of Design in Chicago.

[36] Bertrand Goldberg, "Marina City, Chicago, Illinois," September 1965, 10. Bertrand Goldberg Collection, Ryerson and Burnham Archives, The Art Institute of Chicago.

Rewrapping Marina City (pp. 132–153)

—

Epigraph Linda Legner, "The Goldberg Variations: Space and Structure," *Inland Architect*, January 1974, 8.

1   Ragon, *Goldberg*, 14.

2   Blum, *Oral History of Bertrand Goldberg*, 308.

3   Advertisement for Materialite (lightweight concrete aggregate), *Inland Architect*, November 1961, 2.

4   *Inland Architect*, January 1962, 5.

5   The image was credited to Richard Nickel; Image caption, *Inland Architect*, February 1962, 5.

6   Image caption, *Inland Architect*, April 1962, 5.

7   M. W. N. "Epilogue: People First," *Inland Architect*, January 1974, 22.

8   See Arthur Siegel, Ira Bach, et al., *Chicago's Famous Buildings* (Chicago: University of Chicago Press, 1965).

9   Allan Temko, "Bertrand Goldberg," in *A Guide to 150 Years of Chicago Architecture*, ed. Robert Bruegmann, Sabra Clark, Paul Florian, Douglas Stoker, and Cynthia Weese (Chicago: Chicago Review Press, 1985), 94–105.

10   Ibid., 94.

11   Ibid., 95.

12   Katherine Kuh's precise criticisms are cited: "Moving to Marina City, the lady says the scalloped edges on the outside turn a good idea into unduly romantic exhibitionism...rooms are cramped, interior walls are awkwardly semi-diagonal," "Mabley's Report: Critic Takes City's Sacred Cows Apart!," *Chicago's American*, October 4, 1962.

13   "I have indicated to you in the past Mr. Goldberg makes a great to-do of being one of your students. It is somewhat libelous of him to do so, particularly when talking of this new south side job; and I am not referring to architecture alone." Herbert S. Greenwald's letter to Ludwig Mies van der Rohe, 14 May 1954. Library of Congress, Washington DC. We are indebted to David Dunster for locating this letter.

14   Bertrand Goldberg Archive, "Speeches by Bertrand Goldberg," http://www.justinbraem.com/projects/goldberg/resources/bgspeeches.html.

15   M. W. Newman, "The House of Mies in Chicago," *Inland Architect*, June 1969, 40; Temko, "Bertrand Goldberg," *A Guide to 150 Years of Chicago Architecture*, 94.

16   Stanley Tigerman, "Goldberg, Netsch and Weese: In Exile at Home," *A Guide to 150 Years of Chicago Architecture*, 126–27.

17   Ibid.

18   Ibid., 126.

19   Stanley Tigerman quoted in David Dunlap, "Bertrand Goldberg Dies at 84; Architect Reshaped Chicago," *New York Times*, October 10, 1997.

20   Stuart Cohen, ed., *Chicago Architects* (Chicago: Swallow Press, 1976).

21   Christian Norberg-Schulz, "Chicago: Vision and Image," in *Beyond the International Style: New Chicago Architecture*, ed. Maurizio Casari and Vincenzo Pavan (Chicago: Rizzoli, 1981), 67. Italics in the original.

22   Ibid., 69.

23   Bertrand Goldberg, "Marina City Lecture," Part I, presented by Bertrand Goldberg at the seminar on "Architectural Aspects of Edmonton Civic Centre Plan," September 27, 1959, Bertrand Goldberg Archive, http://www.bertrandgoldberg.org/resources/mclecture_1.html, accessed January 20, 2009.

24   Bertrand Goldberg, "Rich is Right," *Inland Architect*, January/February 1982, 6–15; also reprinted in Ragon, *Goldberg*, 192–97, 199.

25   Goldberg, "Rich is Right," *Goldberg*, 208.

26   Bertrand Goldberg, "The Critical Mass of Urbanism" *Inland Architect*, March–April 1984, 9–10, 12, 47.

27   Bertrand Goldberg, "The Critical Mass of Urbanism," in *Goldberg*, ed. Ragon, 197.

28   Ibid., 192.

29   Ibid., 193.

30   According to Geoffrey Goldberg, Bertrand Goldberg's international network of friends and acquaintances included notable international intellectuals: he knew R. Buckminster Fuller; Françoise Choay gave a copy of her book to Goldberg.

31   Barbara Price, "More about American Housing: Patricia Tindale and Colin Davidson" (report), *Arena: The Architectural Association Journal* 81, no. 893 (June 1965): 25.

32   Richard MacCormac, "Notes on the Role of Form in the Design Process," *Arena: The Architectural Association Journal* 82, no. 912 (May 1967): 280–82.

33   Ibid., 281.

34   Heinrich Klotz, "Bertrand Goldberg, An Architecture for Urbanism," *Architecture and Urbanism*, July 1975, 59–142.

35   Heinrich Klotz, "The Chicago Renaissance," in *Beyond the International Style: New Chicago Architecture*, ed. Maurizio Casari and Vincenzo Pavan (Chicago: Rizzoli, 1981), 31–39.

36   Ibid., 33.

37   Ibid.

38   Robert Venturi, quoted in ibid.

39   Paul Gapp, "Paris Applauds Chicago Architecture," *Chicago Tribune*, November 23, 1983, s1, 9; see also Ante Glibota, "A Note from the Curator," *A Guide to 150 Years of Chicago Architecture*, 4–5.

40   See exhibition catalog for 150 Years of Chicago Architecture: Glibota, "A Note from the Curator," *A Guide to 150 Years of Chicago Architecture*, 5.

41   Ragon, *Goldberg*.

42   Ante Glibota, "City Like a Star," *Goldberg*, 9.

43   Ragon, *Goldberg*, 25.

44   Ibid., 11, 17.

45   Ibid., 11.

46   Bertrand Goldberg, quoted by Ragon in *Goldberg*, 17.

47   Ragon, *Goldberg*, 25.

48   Richard Hoffmann, "Chicago: Study in Power and Clarity" (a conversation with Alvin Boyarsky), *Chicago's American Magazine*, January 9, 1966, 7–8.

49   Alvin Boyarsky quoted in Hoffmann, "Chicago: Study in Power and Clarity," 8.

50   Alvin Boyarsky, "Chicago a la Carte," *AD*, December 1970, 595–640.

51   Ibid., 636.

52   Ibid., 638.

53   Ibid., 622.

54   Ibid.

55   See Materialite advertisement in *Inland Architect*, November 1961, 2.

56   From a Commonwealth Edison advertisement in *Inland Architect*, January 1963, 3.

57   The influence of industrial design on domestic products, such as the influence of airplane cockpits on domestic stoves, was discussed by Pauline Saliga in her essay "To Build a Better Mousetrap: Design in Chicago, 1920–1970" in *Chicago Architecture and Design, 1923–1993*, ed. John Zukowsky (Chicago: The Art Institute of Chicago 2000 (1992)), 265–81.

58   Cross, "The House the Janitors Built," 152.

59   Cover, *National Geographic*, June 1967.

60   Robert Paul Jordan, "Illinois—the City and the Plan," *National Geographic*, June 1967, 745–97.

61   Jordan, "Illinois," 771.

62   Chicago Center for the Print, "Chicago United Air," http://www.prints-posters.com/did680.htm, accessed January 31, 2009.

63   Chicago Center for the Print, "Chicago United Air Mies Buildings," http://www.prints-posters.com/dic712.htm, accessed January 31, 2009.

64   Aeroflot Brochure, 1977, Bertrand Goldberg Collection, Ryerson and Burnham Archives, The Art Institute of Chicago.

65   *Inland Architect*, May 1963.

66   See Wilco, *Yankee Hotel Foxtrot*, produced by Wilco, Nonesuch Records—a Warner Music Group Company, 2002.

67 Peter Maiken, "The Far tottering Master of Parody," *Sunday Tribune*, July 3, 1966.

68 "Corny, but...," Luther Joseph (photographer), *Chicago Daily News*, October 2, 1962.

69 Art Golab, "Repeating the plunge: Car hurls off Marina City for an ad this time," *Chicago Sun-Times*, Monday, October 16, 2006, 4.

70 Ibid.

71 Terry Armour, "Auto/air show—Old Cutlass plunges into Chicago River. Twice." *Chicago Tribune*, Monday, October 16, 2006, http://archives. chicagotribune.com/2006/oct/16/news/ chi-0610160175oct16, accessed January 30, 2009.

72 Beatriz Colomina, *Privacy and Publicity: Modern Architecture and Mass Media* (Cambridge, MA: MIT Press, 1994), 14.

73 Ragon, *Goldberg*, 25.

74 Ibid., 22.

Epilogue (pp. 154–159)

—

Epigraph 1 Blum, *Oral History of Bertrand Goldberg*, 88.

Epigraph 2 Colomina, *Privacy and Publicity*, 14–15.

1 Cohen and Taylor, *American Pharaoh*, 7.

2 "Marina City: Outer-Space Image and Inner-Space Reality," *Architectural Forum*, April 1965, 68–77.

3 Blum, *Oral History of Bertrand Goldberg*, 165; I. M. Pei, with Henry N. Cobb and Araldo A. Cossutta, Apartment helix project, 1949, published in *Architectural Forum*, 1950 and reprinted in Klaus Herdeg, *The Decorated Diagram, Harvard Architecture and the Failure of the Bauhaus Legacy*, (Cambridge, MA: MIT Press, 1983), 17.

4 E-mail from Geoffrey Goldberg to the authors, February 29, 2009.

5 In this way Marina City can be related to the ideas raised by Rem Koolhaas in *Delirious New York*; as with New York skyscrapers, Marina City provided a space for consumer fantasy to be tempered by commercial reality. See Rem Koolhaas, *Delirious New York: A Retroactive Manifesto for Manhattan* (New York: The Monacelli Press, 1994).

6 As William Cronon has written, the emergence of Chicago in the second half of the nineteenth century as the "Second City" of the United States was in large part due to its function as a physical and financial infrastructural hub. See William Cronon, *Nature's Metropolis: Chicago and the Great West* (New York: W.W. Norton, 1991).

7 Colomina, *Privacy and Publicity*, 7.

8 Ibid., 6.

9 Walter Benjamin, "Paris, Capital of the Nineteenth Century," exposé of 1939, in *The Arcades Project*, trans. Howard Eiland and Kevin McLaughlin (Cambridge: The Belknap Press of Harvard University Press, 1999), 19.

10 Benjamin, *The Arcades Project*, 221; Bertrand Goldberg, "Marina City, Chicago, Illinois," September 1965, 10, Bertrand Goldberg Collection, Ryerson and Burnham Archives, The Art Institute of Chicago.

11 Koolhaas, *Delirious New York*, 42.

12 For a detailed account of race and social inequalities in twentieth-century America—including access to space—see Ira Katznelson, *When Affirmative Action Was White: An Untold History of Racial Inequality in Twentieth-Century America* (New York: W. W. Norton and Company, 2005).

13 See Carl Condit's reference to Marina City tenants' racial structure in Condit, *Chicago, 1930–70*, 119.

14 An image of an African American maid, Bertrand Goldberg Collection, Series 6, portfolio 17. Ryerson and Burnham Archives, The Art Institute of Chicago

15 See Carl Condit's reference to class structure of Marina City tenants in Condit, *Chicago, 1930–70*, 119.

16 See, among others, Anja Baumhoff, *The Gendered World of the Bauhaus: The Politics of Power at the Weimar Republic's Premier Art Institute, 1919–1932* (Frankfurt: Peter Lang, 2001); and Katerina Rüedi Ray, *Bauhaus Dream-house: Modernity and Globalization* (New York: Routledge, forthcoming).

→
View from plaza looking up, Marina City (1959–1967), Bertrand Goldberg Associates, Chicago, IL, 1964.
Bertrand Goldberg Archive, Ryerson and Burnham Archives, The Art Institute of Chicaco. Digital File # 200203.081229-320 © The Art Institute of Chicago.

index

Marina City Project Credits

Architects and engineers:
Bertrand Goldberg Associates
Client: Building Service Employees
International Union (Janitors' Union)
Developer: Marks and Company
Structural engineer: Severud-Elstad-
Krueger Associates
General contractor: McHugh
Construction

Subcontractors
Caissons: Case Foundation Company
Concrete: Portland Cement Association
Ready-mixed concrete: Material Service
General construction: Brighton
Construction Company
Roofing: Bennett and Brosseau Roofing
Electrical services: Fischbach,
Moore and Morrissey; Gerson Electric
Construction Company
Electric elevators: Otis
Hydraulic elevators: Gallagher and Spec.
Plumbing: Thomas H. Litvin Plumbing
Company
Ventilation: H. S. Kaiser Company;
Climatemp
Heating and refrigeration: National
Power Company; Economy Plumbing and
Heating Company
Elevator installation: Arrow Contractors;
Clyde Iron Works; Archer Iron Works
Plaster: Mcgurn Brothers